# The Umayyad Caliphate: The History and Legacy of the Second Islamic Kingdom Established After Muhammad's Death

**By Charles River Editors**

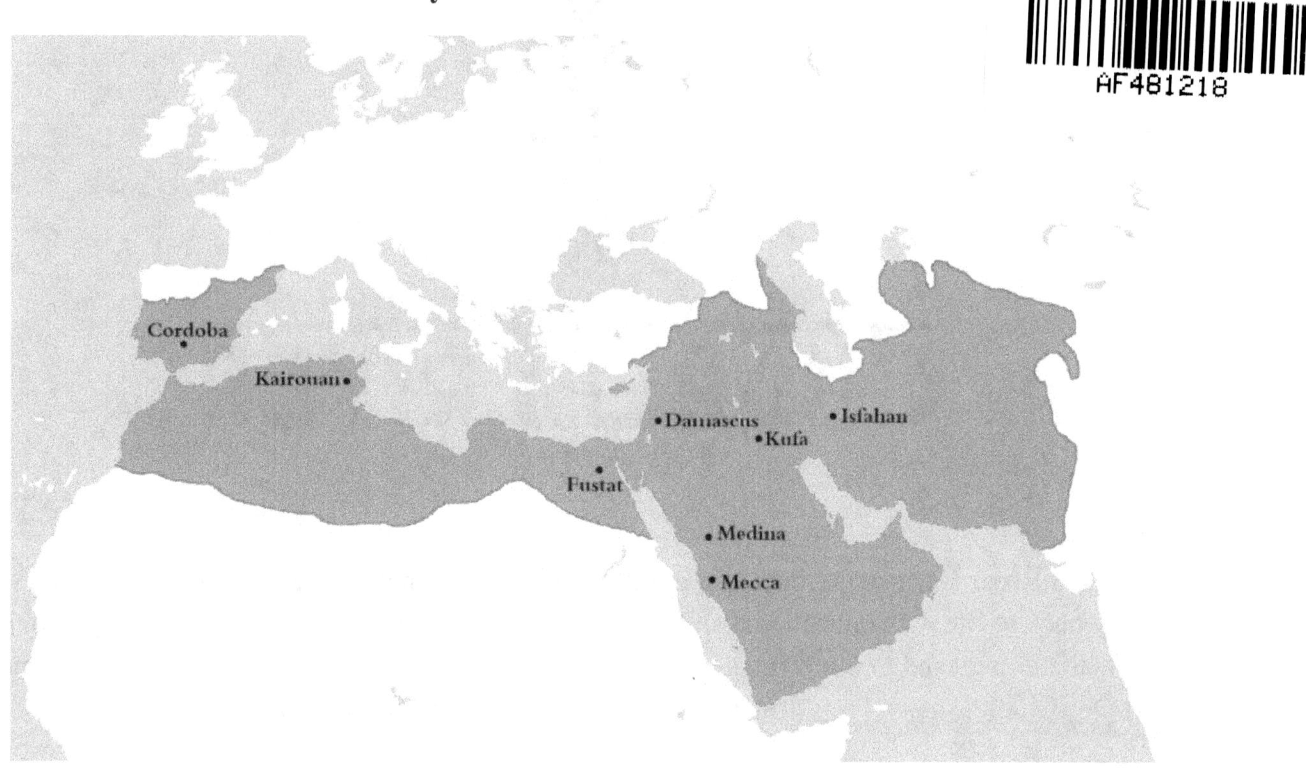


**A map of the Umayyad caliphate at its peak**

# About Charles River Editors

**Charles River Editors** is a boutique digital publishing company, specializing in bringing history back to life with educational and engaging books on a wide range of topics. Keep up to date with our new and free offerings with this 5 second sign up on our weekly mailing list, and visit Our Kindle Author Page to see other recently published Kindle titles.

We make these books for you and always want to know our readers' opinions, so we encourage you to leave reviews and look forward to publishing new and exciting titles each week.

# Introduction

**Classical Numismatic Group, Inc.'s picture of an Umayyad coin**

The split between the two forms of Islam was already in the process of forming upon the death of the Prophet Muhammad. Muhammad had constructed around himself not only a potent new religious movement but also a powerful young state called the Ummah (the "Community" for lack of a better translation). Belonging to the Islamic faith also meant belonging to the Ummah, which was governed by its own laws and had many of its own institutions. In his own lifetime, Muhammad had ruled the Ummah through what sociologists call "charismatic authority," a term coined by Max Weber that is defined as "resting on devotion to the exceptional sanctity, heroism or exemplary character of an individual person, and of the normative patterns or order revealed or ordained by him." Hence, Muslims believe Muhammad ruled because he was uniquely chosen and endowed by God as the exemplar of all humanity, giving him a unique (though not perfect or infallible) ability to govern humanity. This was a holistic form of governance because the Prophet did not simply deliver God's words (what became the Holy Qur'an), nor did he simply pronounce upon court cases and create laws. He did all those things, but he also presented in his own person the embodiment of the best that humanity could aspire to. He was fully human, but the finest, most pious example that humans would ever produce[1].

One of the problems with charismatic authority, as Max Weber recognized and pointed out, is that charismatic authority is fragile because it cannot last beyond the lifespan of the charismatic individual without major changes. As a result, it is often difficult to create continuity after the death of a charismatic leader. Plenty of societies or movements have experienced collapse or massive upheaval after the death of a charismatic leader, such as France after Napoleon and the

---

1   "Max Weber's Conceptualization of Charismatic Authority: Its Influence on Organizational Research" by Jay
    A. Conger in *Leadership Quarterly* V 4, I 3-4, pp 277-288

ancient world after Alexander the Great.

The process of converting a charismatic authority into a more stable, long-term form of government is called "routinizing charisma." In this process, the society attempts to keep some of the legitimizing elements of the deceased leader in place while also creating ways to choose new leaders. This can be agonizing, especially since new leaders rarely live up to or replace the one who has come before. That said, history has provided several successful examples, such as the Roman Empire after Julius Caesar, the Christian Church after Jesus, and the Islamic Republic of Iran after Ayatollah Khomeini.

Amid the upheaval in the Islamic world following Muhammad's death, the Umayyad Caliphate lasted for less than a century, but in that time it managed to become one of the most influential of the major caliphates established following him. Its official existence was from 661-750, and the rulers were the male members of the Umayyad dynasty, roughly translated from Arabic as the "Sons of Umayyah." Its primary base of power was in Syria following the creation of a dynastic, hereditary rule headed by one of Syria's long-lasting governors, Muawiya ibn Abi Sufyan.

Like the other caliphates around that time, the Umayyads existed in a constant state of internal struggle and external conflict. Battles over succession, especially over which lineages possessed the more legitimate claim to power, plagued the early years of the caliphate in Syria. The most significant were the First Muslim Civil War in 661 and the Second Civil War in 680. The official right to become caliph passed between branches of the Umayyad clan, but Syria and Damascus continued to be the main seats of power even as the kingdom expanded to include the Iberian Peninsula, the Transoxiana, the Maghreb, and Sindh.

The Umayyad Caliphate became renowned for being a center of authoritarian power, education, and cultural development. The population was multiethnic and consisted of local peoples conquered throughout Africa, Europe, and Asia, including regional Christians and Jews. At its greatest extent, the empire extended over an area of 4,300,000 sq. miles, with over 33,000,000 residents. It was one of the largest known empires in history, even considering modern developments, and a precursor to the Golden Age of Islam.

Scholars throughout history have remained divided on the best way to interpret the legacy left by the Umayyads. On the one hand, they were able to unite a massive array of people and exert control over millions of square miles. On the other hand, they became infamous for their treatment of religious and ethnic minorities, were seen as turning away from God in favor of material excess, and managed to be overthrown by the millions they isolated through their policies. Through it all, they offered lessons for future Muslim kingdoms about the dangers of trying to combine religious beliefs with secular administration in a diverse world, and ultimately, the Umayyads would be replaced by the far more intelligent and crafty Abbasids, who managed to wield powerful tools like propaganda to undermine their opponents.

It remains a subject of modern debate how to best understand the Umayyads, but there is no doubt they were one of the most influential of the early medieval empires and paved the way for future Islamic caliphates to wield impressive amounts of influence throughout the Middle East. *The Umayyad Caliphate: The History and Legacy of the Second Islamic Kingdom Established After the Prophet's Death* chronicles the caliphate's life and accomplishments, and the massive impact it left on the world. Along with pictures of important people, places, and events, you will learn about the Umayyad Caliphate like never before.

## The Rashidun Caliphate

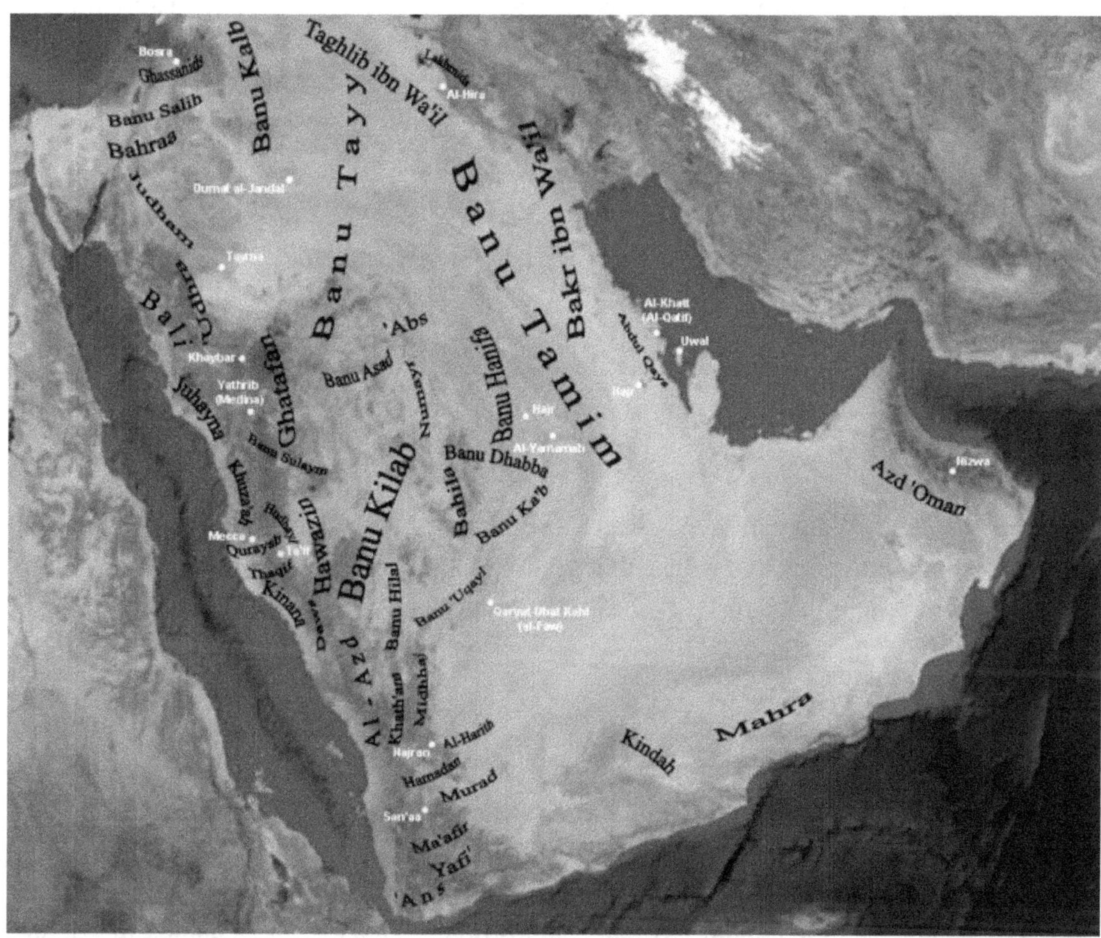

**The Arabian Peninsula and the names of various tribes during Muhammad's life**

When Muhammad died, the Ummah realized he could not be truly replaced and that there would never again be a man like him. That said, the Ummah hoped to find a leader that was still significantly superior to the ordinary man, and the most obvious candidates for superior people were the Prophet's family. Was there some way that the special qualities of Muhammad could be found amongst the members of his close family? Was there some special teaching or insight that Muhammad passed on to his family? Were Muhammad's teachings and the blessings of God only to be found within the Qur'an and the emulation of the life of the Prophet and therefore available equally to all Muslims? If there was something special about Muhammad, then special consideration should be given to the Prophet's family in the political life of the new Islamic state. However, if the leaders of the Ummah should be chosen based on their knowledge of the Qur'an, their piety, and their ability to administer and defend the community, then there was no need to turn just to Muhammad's family for leadership.

Ultimately, those who believed in a special place for the role of the Prophet's family became the Shias, while those who believed that all Muslims were equally capable in the eyes of God became the Sunnis. Even today, however, many rulers claim lineage to the Prophet as a form of legitimacy, including in Sunni states such as the modern Hashemite dynasty in Jordan.[2]

Within the Shia position - that there is something unique about the Prophet's line that gives them a special ability to rule - there is an important division that was not immediately apparent after the Prophet's death: is this uniqueness something that is born within them, or is it a special knowledge which comes from either a secret teaching or from insights gained from prolonged intimacy with Muhammad? This is important because if it is knowledge, then it can be codified and taught to those who are not his descendants, and it can also be lost by those who are.

While Muslims have continued to debate this issue, the Prophet and the Qur'an are ambivalent on it. On the one hand, there is a strong assertion of the equality of all Muslims, including the following passages:

> "O Mankind, We created you from a single (pair) of a male and a female and made you into nations and tribes, that you may know each other. Verily the most honored of you in the sight of God is he who is the most righteous of you (Quran 49:13)."

> "O people, Remember that your Lord is One. An Arab has no superiority over a non-Arab nor a non-Arab has any superiority over an Arab; also a black has no superiority over white, nor a white has any superiority over black, except by piety and good action (Taqwa). Indeed the best among you is the one with the best character (Taqwa). Listen to me. Did I convey this to you properly? People responded, Yes. O messenger of God, The Prophet then said, then each one of you who is there must convey this to everyone not present. (Excerpt from the Prophet's Last Sermon as in Baihiqi)"

> "The Prophet said: Let people stop boasting about their ancestors. One is only a pious believer or a miserable sinner. All men are sons of Adam, and Adam came from dust (Abu Dawud, Tirmidhi)."

On the other hand, these eminent sources also had something to say in support of the other side. There are a number of Hadith (sayings or teachings of the Prophet) that the Shia hold up to support their claims about Ali's special status as the heir-apparent of Muhammad. The first is the Hadith of the Pond of Kumm, when the Prophet gave a sermon in which he discussed how he would meet them in heaven: "I will ask you about the two weighty things that I have left for you when you come to me to see how you dealt with them. The greater weighty thing is Allah's book—the Holy Qur'an. One end is in Allah's hand and the other is in your hands. Keep it and you will not deviate. That other weighty thing is my family and my descendants."[3]

---

Another important argument is found in the Hadith of the Cloak, a story in which the Prophet wrapped Ali, Fatima and their two sons Husayn and Hasan in his cloak and declared that they were sinless and composed his family (and by extension were his inheritors). While there are a number of others, one that will come up later is the Hadith of the Twelve Successors, in which the Prophet taught that there would only be 12 legitimate Caliphs after him and a plethora of false caliphs, and that after the last of his successors the earth will end[4].

These religious interpretations remain an important part of the Sunni-Shia debate today, but in the early political context of the upheaval after the Prophet's death, these debates were not philosophical but were instead connected to different candidates for the mantle of Muhammad's successor. In fact, it is altogether possible that the candidates existed and were well-known before these justifications were developed to support them. Upon Muhammad's death, the debate was between two individuals: Abdullah ibn Abi Qhuhafah (commonly known as "Abu Bakr") and `Alī ibn Abī Ṭālib ("Ali").

---

3    The Sunnah of the Prophet can be found in English at: http://sunnah.com/
4    *Muhammad: A Prophet for Our Time* by Karen Armstrong (2007)

**A 16<sup>th</sup> century depiction of Abu Bakr in Mecca**

Both men were already eminent within the Ummah and featured prominently in the histories of the life of the Prophet. Abu Bakr was the father-in-law of the Prophet and - like Muhammad - was a merchant based in the city of Mecca before Muhammad declared his Prophethood. He was outside Mecca traveling with a caravan as Muhammad first announced his new faith, and when he returned to the city, Abu Bakr was the first convert to Islam from outside Muhammad's own family. This was a major step because Muhammad called upon Muslims to abandon narrow clan ties for connection to the larger Ummah, and Abu Bakr served as one of the Prophet's closest advisors. While his daughter Aisha was married to Muhammad, since the Arabs were (and remain) patrilineal, this meant that Aisha entered Muhammad's family (male line), but it also meant Muhammad did not enter Abu Bakr's family. As a result, Abu Bakr is not considered to be a kinsman of the Prophet.

Ali, on the other hand, was family. The cousin of the Prophet on the male line, he was also married to the Prophet's most beloved daughter, Fatima. According to Islamic histories, Ali was born in the Kaaba, the sacred shrine at the heart of the holy city of Mecca, and he was the first man to convert to Islam upon hearing Muhammad's message. Like Abu Bakr, Ali had served as the Prophet's lieutenant, especially in military matters. Ali had regularly led the Muslim troops into battle.

**A 16th century depiction of Ali leading soldiers in battle**

When the Prophet died in 632, choosing Muhammad's successor was a decision ultimately made by the Sahabah, a term used for the body of individuals who had known the Prophet during his life (in English, it is often called the "Companions of the Prophet"). It is difficult from such a distance to say exactly why the Sahabah preferred Abu Bakr over Ali, but there are several plausible arguments, and it's safe to assume that even Abu Bakr's supporters would have had different reasons for their allegiance to him. One is that Abu Bakr was considerably older than Ali, and in the strictly hierarchical society of Medieval Arabia, age and experience were vitally important. There is an old Arab saying that men are not wise until the age of 40,[5] and Ali was only 32 or 25 (depending on which source on his birth one reads).[6]

Another possible reason for excluding Ali from the center of power may have been based on the fact he was a member of the Prophet's family. Early Islam was a religion that placed a great emphasis on egalitarianism, especially since the Prophet and the Qur'an called upon Muslims to reject their old ties of clan, tribe, and ethnicity. It may have been that the Sahabah wanted precisely to avoid creating a hereditary dynasty within the Prophet's family as a supreme rejection of the old clannishness[7].

Whatever the reasons, Abu Bakr was chosen to become "caliph," a shortened form of the title "Khalifat Rasul Allah" ("Successors to the Messenger of God"). The Caliph inherited all of the Prophet's political authority and much of spiritual power as well.

Since the election of Abu Baker in 623, there have been hundreds of individuals from close to a dozen dynasties that have claimed the Caliphate, but only the first four are widely considered by Sunnis to have inherited the true spiritual mantle of the Prophet. These four men, all of whom were Sahabah (Companions of the Prophet in his life), are called the "Rashidun" (or "Rightly Guided" Caliphs), and their government is referred to as the Rashidun or Patriarchal Caliphate (632-661).

After the Prophet's death in 632, the Caliphate controlled the Arabian Peninsula, which today consists of Saudi Arabia, Yemen, Oman, the United Arab Emirates, and Qatar, but it expanded during the Rashidun period with the conquests of today's Iraq, Syria, Israel, the Palestinian territories, Jordan, Persia, Armenia, Egypt, Cyprus, Lebanon, Azerbaijan, Kuwait, and Bahrain, as well as portions of Afghanistan, Turkmenistan, Turkey, and Libya.

However, it was also during this period that the division between Sunnis and Shias was taking shape. Initially, it consisted of a political division, with the proto-Shia as something akin to a loyal opposition; they supported the overall system of the Caliphate, obeyed the Caliph's rulings and were pious Muslims, but they believed that Ali was the better candidate and may have had strong opinions about the special place of the family of the Prophet in public affairs.

---

5    This is a widespread belief in Arab lands, and was confirmed by the fact that Muhammad's Prophethood did not begin until his fortieth year.

6    "The Caliphate" in *Islam: Faith, Culture, History* (2002). By Paul Lunde. DK Publishing.

7    *No God But God: The Origins, Evolution and Future of Islam* by Resa Aslan (2011). Random House

One point of conflict during Abu Bakr's rule was over the oasis of Fadak. Located close to Mecca, it was one of the Muslim army's earliest conquests and had been under the direct control of Muhammad during his lifetime. At his death, his daughter Fatima (Ali's wife) claimed that it had been owned by Muhammad due to the right of conquest and that he had willed it to her. Abu Bakr, on the other hand, denied this claim and stated that a Prophet of God could not own property. Thus, Abu Bakr asserted that after the Prophet's death, the lands under his control reverted back to public ownership and were to be managed by the Caliph. While Fatima assented to Abu Bakr's ruling, she was furious over it, and it created a rift between her family and the Caliph. After this event, Ali and Fatima retreated from the public eye to become farmers, but before she died a few months later, Fatima gave a rousing speech in the Mosque of the Prophet before the Caliph and the assembled Sahabah in which she denounced their government as turning its back upon true Islam and praising her husband as an alternative. This event, known as the "Fadakyiah Sermon," can be considered the intellectual foundation of Shia Islam, and it continues to resonate with Shias today.[8]

---

8   For a Shia interpretation of these events, read: http://en.shafaqna.com/etrat/item/26306-fadak-an-outcry-beyond-a-bequest.html

**A medieval depiction of Muhammad giving Fatima in marriage to Ali**

Fadak continued to emerge as a point of contention throughout the Rashidun Caliphate and became a symbol of the shoddy treatment that Shias believe the family of Ali and Fatima - the true heirs of the Prophet - received at the hands of jealous, power-hungry proto-Sunni Caliphs. It still continues to be a rallying cry for those who seek to restore the birthright of Ali's line, such as the radical Shia Fadak satellite television station, which broadcasts anti-Sunni rhetoric from London.

Abu Bakr only ruled for two years, and after his death, he was replaced by his handpicked successor, the famously stern Umar (also written Omar). Umar addressed Muslims in the wake of Abu Bakr's death and said, "O ye faithful! Abu Bakr is no more amongst us. He has the satisfaction that he has successfully piloted the ship of the Muslim state to safety after negotiating the stormy sea. He successfully waged the apostasy wars, and thanks to him, Islam is now supreme in Arabia. After Abu Bakr, the mantle of the Caliphate has fallen on my shoulders. I swear it before God that I never coveted this office. I wished that it would have devolved on some other person more worthy than me. But now that in national interest, the responsibility for leading the Muslims has come to vest in me, I assure you that I will not run away from my post, and will make an earnest effort to discharge the onerous duties of the office to the best of my capacity in accordance with the injunctions of Islam. Allah has examined me from you and you from me, In the performance of my duties, I will seek guidance from the Holy Book, and will follow the examples set by the Holy Prophet and Abu Bakr. In this task I seek your assistance. If I follow the right path, follow me. If I deviate from the right path, correct me so that we are not led astray."

Succeeding to the caliphate in 634, Umar ruled until 644 and profoundly shaped the emerging Muslim state largely through his skill as a jurist and lawmaker. Under Umar, the Caliphate continued to expand, conquering the Levant, Egypt, coastal Libya and - crucially for the future history of Shias - the entire Persian Empire. Umar attempted some reconciliation with the extended family of Ali, but he still maintained Abu Bakr's position on Fatima's contested inheritance at the oasis of Fadak.

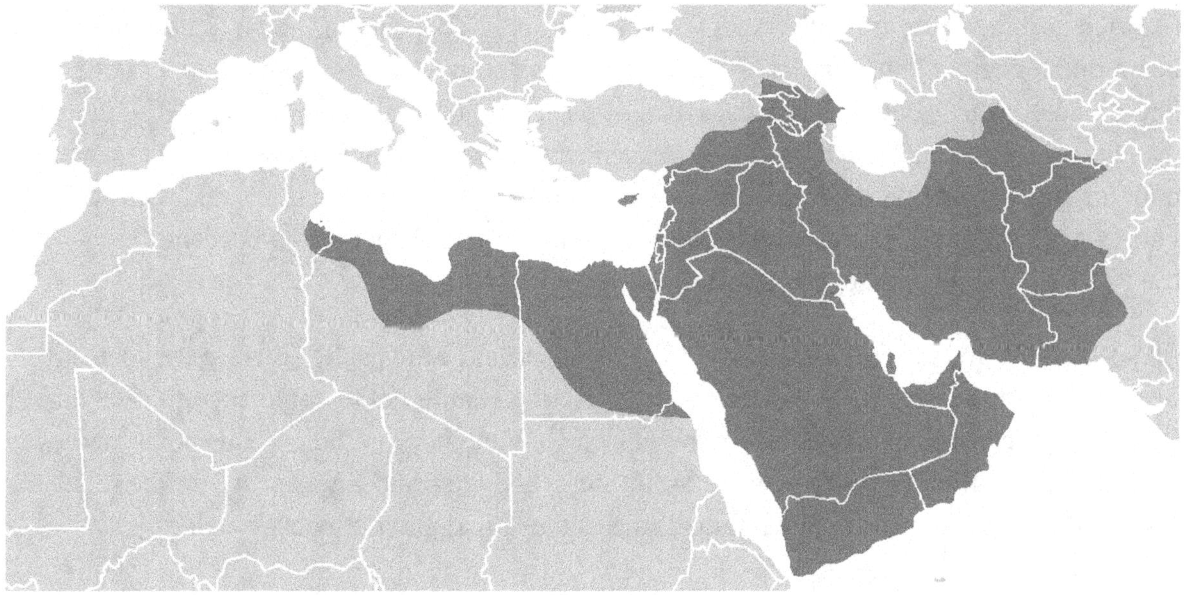

**Mohammad Adil's map of the expansion of the Rashidun Caliphate**

For the Sunnis, Umar has gone down in history as the greatest of the Faqih, an expert in "fiqh" (Islamic jurisprudence). During this period, the Ummah went through major changes as the number of Sahabah (Companions of the Prophet - those who heard Muhammad speak and had direct knowledge of his teachings) was decreasing both overall (as people like Abu Bakr died) and as a percentage of the overall population. This meant that the direct lessons of the Prophet and his example were becoming increasingly more difficult to teach, and as the Empire expanded, there was a greater need to apply Islamic law to an ever-growing number of cultural contexts. Umar and the scholars of his period began the process of collecting and codifying the Hadith (teachings of the Prophet) and creating a body of organized, universally-applicable laws for the new state[9].

While Sunnis and Shias differ on their interpretations of the Hadith, these collected sayings and acts of the Prophet are central to all forms of Islam and demonstrate how the word of God - the Qur'an - is applied in the life and words of a pious man as near perfect as a human could be. However, since the Prophet himself never wrote up a book of his teachings (Muslims consider the Qur'an a recitation from God given word-for-word to the Prophet), after his death there was a chaotic jumble of ideas. On top of that, the memories of the Sahabah began to falter as they grew older, and some Sahabah and non-Sahabah began to invent spurious "teachings."

What scholars have done for generations is collect and write down these Hadith and then sifted through the collections, examining the chain of oral transmission and the character of the transmitters to determine which Hadith they gave weight to. This also means that there are numerous similar (but often subtly or even dramatically) different versions of the same tale. The Sunni tend to be relatively liberal in accepting Hadith as their basic assumption; if a Sahabah reported a Hadith, they trust its veracity unless that individual can be shown to have abandoned Islam or the chain of transmission to the recorder was faulty. The Shia, on the other hand, interpret all of the Hadith through the prism of the treatment of the *Ahl al-Bayt* ("The People of the House"), a general term used for the descendents of Muhammad but used in Shia contexts only for Ali, Fatima and their descendents. Those among the minority that sided with Ali and Fatima against Abu Bakr and Umar in their disputes on inheritance and precedence are viewed by Shia faqih as the only legitimate sources of Hadith.

That said, during the era of Umar - before the open Sunni-Shia split - there were no such divisions made, so Muslim authorities were collecting Hadith not to compete with each other but to gather up the holy teachings before they faded from memory. In fact, at this point there were no theological differences between the proto-Sunni and the proto-Shia except for the relative importance they placed upon the political role of the Ahl al-Bayt, especially Ali.

In 644, Umar was murdered by a stab wound from a slave, and the fact that this slave was of Persian origin became a point of Sunni-Shia friction centuries later after Persia converted to Shi'ism under the Safavids. On his deathbed, Umar appointed a committee of six men to find his successor, and this committee included Ali and the eventual choice, Uthman ibn Affan. All six were part of the aging cohort of Sahabah and had been prominent political actors throughout the Prophet's reign and the succeeding caliphs.

9    *Islam: Faith, Culture, History* (2002). By Paul Lunde. DK Publishing. Pp 48-49

The committee had to come to consensus, and according to legends, Umar ordered his son to kill any single member of the committee who held out against consensus. One of the six, Zubayr, backed Ali, and another, Sa'd ib Abi Waqas, supported Uthman. The remaining candidate/committee member, Abdur Rahman, withdrew from the running and was appointed arbiter. The final committee member, Talhah, was not present because he had been in a distant part of the empire when Umar died.

Eventually, the committee gathered before the Ummah at the Friday night prayers in the Mosque of the Prophet in Mecca, and when Abdur Rahman gave his support to Uthman, it forced Ali's hand. The committee announced it had reached a consensus, but Shias continue to maintain that Ali never accepted Uthman because he knew that the Prophet had appointed him as the only legitimate successor.

Regardless, upon his ascension, Uthman continued the military campaigns of his predecessor and pushed Islamic armies into Khorasan (today's northwestern Afghanistan), Balochistan (southern Pakistan), Armenia, and northern Africa. His rule lasted for 12 years, but while the first half of his reign was peaceful, the second half witnessed growing discord that eventually led to open revolt. The Shia argue that even in the time of Uthman, the later tendencies of the Sunni caliphs towards rule not as the first among equals but as dynastic monarchs was evident. Uthman had appointed his family members to governorships, accepted rich gifts, and used monies from the public treasury for himself, all of which flew in the face of the rigid egalitarianism of the previous rulers.

All of the discord culminated in 656 with the assassination of Uthman and unrest across the empire. The assassination itself was a dramatic event known as the "Siege of Uthman," which consisted of angry citizens/rebels from outlying areas converging on Mecca with a set of demands for Uthman. Central to their complaints was Uthman's appointment of his extended family as governors. The exact events are still unclear, but it is possible that documents were faked by his cousin Marwan (who would later be Caliph) that ordered the rebel leaders executed. Ali was called upon by Uthman to intercede, but his attempts at negotiations failed, so the rebels continued to besiege Uthman within his home. The siege was a slow-motion affair of many days and largely without open bloodshed - Ali was even able to bring water to the Caliph – but in the end, rebels led by Muhammed ibn Abu Bakr broke in and killed the Caliph[10].

Not surprisingly, the nature of these revolts and the assassination is clouded by centuries of assertions by Sunni and Shia, especially since the development of radical Wahhabi Sunni theology in the 19th and 20th centuries. The Wahhabis (who are discussed in much greater detail in the final chapter) argue that the decline of Islam is due to the corruptions of the true faith, in particular by the Shia, who they view as heretical. These theologians and historians argue that

---

10  "'Uthman ibn 'Affan" in *The Encyclopedia Britannica* accessed online at:
   http://www.britannica.com/EBchecked/topic/620653/Uthman-ibn-Affan

the Caliph was brought down by a Jewish figure named Abd Allah ibn Saba᾽ al-Ḥimyarī, and that he was funded by external enemies of the Islamic empire to sow divisions within the faith and undermine the Caliphate. They argue that the theological roots of Shi'ism comes from this individual, who led a revolt movement that assassinated Uthman in order to put the corrupted Ali on the throne and end the Empire's expansion. The Wahhabis point to connections between some of the rebels and Ali, including Muhammed ibn Abu Bakr, who was Ali's adopted son[11] and became a general for him when he was Caliph.

Shia historians, on the other hand, claim that Abd Allah ib Saba᾽ al-Ḥimyarī is a fictional character created to disparage the Shia by claiming that their theology is Jewish in origin. This is considered an especially damning charge after the creation of the state of Israel in 1948. Moreover, the Shias insist that Abd Allah ib Saba᾽ al-Ḥimyarī was concocted to place the blame for the end of the Rashidun Caliphate on their betrayal[12]. Instead, they argue that the Caliphate lost its path when it appointed a figure other than Ali as Caliph in the first place, and that the creeping growth of this corruption could be seen in Uthman's increasingly monarchic tendencies.

In 656, Uthman's death finally made Ali the leader of the Caliphate, and respect for Ali and for his caliphate is the last point of historical commonality between the Sunnis and the Shia before their trajectories took them in different directions. Changes had swept the Ummah (community of Muslims); the Prophet had died 34 years ago, and the community of his Companions - the Sahabah - were vanishing and losing their control over social and religious life. Thus, Ali took over an empire in the throes of revolt but managed to hold onto power for the next five years.

Immediately after the death of Uthman, the rebel factions declared Ali to be their Caliph, but Ali turned them down at first. As a result, the rebels demanded a Caliph be appointed, so the remaining members of the committee that appointed Uthman and were in Medina - Ali, Talhah, Zubayr[13] - met together in the Mosque of the Prophet with others of the Sahabah. This committee eventually appointed Ali the new Caliph, but there would be debate among those involved, as well as historians, as to whether this was done willingly or by force. Either way, the events at Medina were not unchallenged by those opposed to Ali, and conflicting rumors spread like wildfire across the Empire about the nature of Uthman's death and the appointment of Ali. The opposition gathered around Aisha, the Prophet's wife, and then around Muawiyah, the second cousin of Uthman and Marwan and the governor of Syria in Damascus[14]. Another lesser faction was based in Egypt around the governor of that province, Amr ibn al-As.

In one form or another, the First Civil War (called a "Fitna") consumed Ali's reign and

---

11  The first Caliph, Abu Bakr, was his biological father.
12   For a summary of the evidence in the debate, read: "Authentic References and Case Research of ibn al Saba's Existence" accessed online at: http://makashfa.wordpress.com/2012/12/16/authentic-references-and-case-research-of-ibn-al-sabas-existance/
13  Sa'd ib Abi Waqas, was governing Persia at the time.
14  He was not, however, one of Uthman's nepotistic appointments as he had been given his position by Umar.

ultimately brought about his death. Around him gathered a group of loyal followers who became known as the *Shī'atu 'Alī*, a term that means Party of Ali, and over time, "Shiatu Ali" became shortened to "Shia," the term that continues to be used today. Hence, it can be said that while the roots of Shi'ism go back to even before the death of the Prophet, the Shia become an identifiable political group upon Ali's succession.

The first open battle in the conflict was the Battle of the Camel on November 7, 656. When Muawiyah sent his word that he would not recognize Ali, Aisha, Talhah and Zubayr (who were on pilgrimage together) traveled to Medina to ask Ali not to attack Muawiyah but to instead hunt the killers of Uthman. When they learned that Ali was not hunting the killers, they allied with Marwan and his kinfolk (the Umayyad clan). Ali learned of their movements and summoned groups from the Iraqi city of Kufa to aid him.

When the two armies met, it seemed that conflict would be avoided once all of the main parties agreed to a truce and settlement. However, during that night, unknown hotheads attacked the camps, sparking wider fighting. Both Zubayr and Talhah refused to participate, but Zubayr was killed by one of his soldiers and Talhah was killed by Marwan. The battle was fierce and included thousands on both sides, with the focus being on the capture of Aisha on her camel. Aisha eventually surrendered and was pardoned by Ali, and Marwan was captured.

**A medieval depiction of the Battle of the Camel**

This solidified Ali's control over the heartland of the Caliphate but left the Umayyad clan and Muawiyah in rebellion in Syria. Thus, the civil war continued to rage as Ali attempted to conquer the rebellious provinces and hold the Caliphate together. Finally, the two armies met in 657 at the Battle of Siffin on the banks of the Euphrates River near present day Raqqa in Syria.[15] Once

15 There were roots of earlier conflicts here. The Byzantine and Persian Empires had long maintained proxy states in Syria and Iraq (respectively) and the two groups - both Arabic speaking - were old and bitter rivals even when

again, they were slow to engage and preferred to attempt to settle their difficulties, but even though the two sides held off for months to negotiate, fighting eventually broke out. Thousands died on each side and both leaders retreated, so the conflict remained unresolved.

Eventually, Ali agreed to Muawiyah's call for arbitration according to the laws set down in the Qur'an, but when word spread that Ali agreed to negotiations as if Muawiyah was an equal, a faction of his most radical and fiercest supporters broke off and retreated to southern Iraq, becoming a sect called the Kharijites. In the end, Ali left the arbitration greatly weakened, making Muawiyah the symbolic victor. Ali retreated to his wartime capital in Iraqi Kufa, and Muawiyah headed to Damascus, where he was declared Caliph in 658. There were other campaigns in the aftermath of Siffin, but Muawiyah's influence gradually began to expand. Ali was further weakened by battles in 659 against the Kharijites, which eventually led to his assassination by the Kharijites in the Great Mosque of Kufa in 661.[16]

Even as the Sunnis and Shias continued to split, there were still some overlaps between the two, and there have always been periods of shared history that they agree upon. One example is the 4th Shia Imam Muhammad ibn Ali (677–732), who, despite being the head of the "Party of Ali," became a well-respected scholar in Sunni circles as well. However, the simmering conflict between the Umayyad Dynasty and their Shia challengers to the throne exploded during the reign of the Caliph Yazid I, the son of Muawiyah I who reigned from 661-680. When Yazid came to power, he represented a new element in the religious and political life of the Empire; he was a ruler born after the death of the Prophet (and thus was not one of the Companions), and he was the first to be appointed to his position by filling his father's seat. Ali's son Hasan had ruled as Caliph for a short period during the conflict after his father's death, but this had not been over the majority of the Caliphate and was barely long enough for him to surrender. Thus, Yazid I came to represent the political corruption that was seeping into the Caliphate.

Ali's elder son, Hasan, had died in 670, so he did not live to see Yazid come to power, but his younger brother, Hussein (also spelled Husayn), did. In 680, Hussein had been the prominent leader of the Shia for 10 years, and he refused to accept Yazid as Caliph, noting that the peace treaty that he had signed with Muawiyah to end the Fitna had expressly prohibited the Umayyads from appointing one of their own as successor. Hussein was 54 at the time, while Yazid was only 34, and he had been one of the Companions of the Prophet. Furthermore he was mentioned by name in the Hadith, and the Prophet was said to have given him special favor. His most important ally at the time was ibn Zubayr, the grandson of Abu Bakr (the first Rasidun Caliph).

Hussein gathered his allies at Mecca, far from the center of Umayyad power in Damascus but at the heart of the old traditional power bases. The people of Kufa, Ali's old capital, heard of

---

absorbed into the Islamic Empire. Hence, when Muawiyah went into rebellion in Syria, many Iraqis from Kufa were more than willing to join the fight against him.

16  "'Ali" in the *Encyclopedia Britannica* accessed online at:
    http://www.britannica.com/EBchecked/topic/15223/Ali

Hussein's revolt and sent word to Mecca that they were ready to join the revolution. They further encouraged him to make Kufa his capital, and against the advice of ibn Zubayr, Hussein gathered his family and companions and headed towards Kufa.

Meanwhile, Yazid moved quickly to consolidate his power, including sending his lieutenants to Kufa to depose the local governor and attempt to control the city's crowds. He also sent armies to the roads between Mecca and Kufa, anticipating Hussein's movements. Once Yazid's forces encountered Hussein on the road, there was a tense period of negotiation and wary watchful encampments. According to Shia accounts, Hussein's party shared water with the Umayyad soldiers, but they refused to return mercy by forcing Hussein to encamp far from water sources and then killing Hussein's younger brother, Abbas. Both sides agree that the truce broke down, resulting in the Battle of Karbala, during which Hussein and 72 of his followers were killed and decapitated. The bodies of the dead were left in the desert, but the soldiers returned with the heads and the captured women and children to Damascus to deliver them to Yazid. In the process, Hussein's sister Zaynab rose to prominence by denouncing the Caliph and protecting the honor of the surviving female members of the family.

**A depiction of important figures at the Battle of Karbala, with the central figure being Abbas**

These shocking events were seared into the consciences of the people of Kufa and all of the Shia, not to mention many Sunnis who have come to view the Umayyad Dynasty as corrupt and tyrannical. The annual observance of Hussein's death is called Ashura, meaning "Tenth," referring to the fact that it is the 10th day of the Muslim month of Muharram. For the Shia, it is seen as a day commemorating triumph over, and opposition to, tyrannical government. According to legend, the first commemoration of Hussein's death was held in the prison in

Damascus and led by Zaynab, who has since become a symbol of strength, resistance to oppression, and piety.

The Battle of Karbala led to the rise of the Umayyad Caliphate, but eventually, a mosque – the Imam Husayn Shrine – was built in Karbala over the grave of Hussein, and it became the focal point of annual Ashura pilgrimages. Even outside of Karbala, Ashura has become a time when Shia march through the streets of their hometowns carrying banners, funeral biers, and performing an act called a Matam, which involves beating one's breast either with the open palm or holding an object like a knife or a chain, in lamentation for the dead. Ashura is the most obvious, public, and controversial marker of Shia identity, and the annual celebration of Ashura is always fraught with controversy and conflict. For one, it is a symbol of Shia-ness in nations where the Shia are often a minority (such as in India or Lebanon) or an oppressed majority (such as in Saddam Hussein's Iraq or contemporary Bahrain). On the other side, it is a symbol of opposition to oppression and has become a rallying point for dissent against tyrants (such as the Shah of Iran, Saddam Hussein or the government of Pakistan).

**The Imam Husayn Shrine in Karbala, Iraq**

## The Umayyad Caliphate's Social Structure

Within the caliphate were four distinct social classes which controlled where a person could live, their position in society, and whether they were subjected to increased taxation and limited rights. These four classes were the Muslim Arabs, the Muslim non-Arabs, the *dhimmis*, and the slaves.

Not surprisingly, the Muslim Arabs dominated society and held the majority of significant positions within the caliphate, including administrators, governors, tax collectors, religious leaders, and prosperous traders. Despite Islamic teachings which stated all Muslims were equal, the Muslim Arabs did not mix or mingle with their non-Arab counterparts and kept themselves walled away in separate districts.

Underneath the Arabs were the Muslim non-Arabs, often individuals or native peoples who converted to Islam from another religion. These people were supposed to receive the same rights, protections, and opportunities as their Arab counterparts, but this was not the case. Almost no members of this social class managed to climb to significant positions in the military or government, and none were chosen as religious leaders.

The inequality between the Arab and non-Arab Muslims provided a constant form of strife and social unrest. The Umayyad Caliphate was successful in spreading Islam across North Africa, into Asia, and into the Iberian Peninsula of Europe, but as the years passed, more and more of the population was composed of non-Arab Muslims who demanded the rights they were promised for converting. Unfortunately, the governors did not want to acknowledge the converts, as they were making money by taxing them for following another religion. In other words, many administrators in the caliphate continued to treat the non-Arab Muslims as *dhimmis*.

*Dhimmis* were the third social class and constituted members of the population who refused to convert to Islam. They formed a large portion of the population and were often adherents of Christianity, Judaism, Zoroastrianism, and other local religions. Since they did not become Muslims, the *dhimmis* were forced to pay special religious taxes like the *jizya*. By paying, the *dhimmis* could live in relative peace as legally recognized second class citizens but were relegated to the poorer quarters. Despite their situation, many great Christian and Jewish theologians emerged from the Umayyad Caliphate and contributed greatly to the understanding of their religions.

The final class consisted of slaves. They were not considered citizens and possessed limited rights and protections, with their lives and safety often forfeit and in the control of their masters. The vast majority of slaves were captives taken during the long period of expansion and conquest of the Umayyads.

No empire would be complete or successful without an effective administration that established communication across the land, collected taxes, and carried out justice, but when the Umayyad Caliphate first developed, it struggled to form a cohesive system. The first four caliphs were tasked with developing a stable administration, and since it was one of the first Islamic states, the rulers did not have many regional empires on which to base their new caliphate. Instead, the caliphs chose to emulate the practices of the nearby Byzantine Empire, which possessed strong administrative institutions and powerful branches of government. These four branches were of political affairs, tax collection, religious administration, and military affairs.

To better administer to their territory, the Umayyads split the empire into multiple provinces, although the borders changed significantly over time. Each province had a governor appointed directly by the caliph. The governor then controlled the region and was responsible for all other civil or religious leaders in the domain, including religious officials and civil administrators. Even generals were supposed to adhere to the governor, but military leaders operated with more license than other officials. One of the most influential areas would be Khorasan, or the eastern territories. Although the Umayyad Caliphate did expand significantly to the west and managed to conquer the majority of the Iberian Peninsula, administrating such far areas would always be a major challenge.

The provinces economically operated with some independence from the central Umayyad administration. Local expenses were paid for with taxes gathered from the regional population and the remainder was sent to the central government in Damascus – although the location of the primary branch of government shifted several times throughout the years. Because the Umayyad Caliphate was plagued with civil wars and succession crises, many of the governors did not send their tax revenue to the central administration and were able to amass personal fortunes.[17]

When it came to the operation of the government, the original intent of the Umayyads was to limit positions of power to qualified Arab Muslims. However, as the empire rapidly expanded, the pool of qualified Arabs decreased significantly. Eventually, the caliphs were forced to let local government workers and administrators maintain their positions in conquered provinces to better manage the new territory. This meant Arab Muslims slowly lost some of their prestige in the empire, and also that administrative documents started to be written in languages other than Arabic, such as Persian, Coptic, and even Greek. It was not until the 8th century that all government work became consolidated and written in Arabic throughout the territories.[18]

Another issue the administration faced was attempting to decide upon a currency. Since the Umayyads spread and started to encompass and include other civilizations in their empire, they needed to find a way to unify the currency while balancing many different monetary systems. As a solution, the Umayyad Caliphate once again copied the nearby Byzantines and even used Byzantine copper and gold coins until monetary reforms were implemented around 700. The first Muslim coins in history were not minted until post-700, and these were created in Damascus. Gold coins were dinars and silver coins were dirhams. No individual copper coins were printed

---

[17] Hugh Kennedy, *The Prophet and the Age of the Caliphates: The Islamic Near East from the 6th to the 11th Century* (Second ed.). Harlow: Longman, 2004.
[18] Ibid.

at this point.

Finally, the central administration was divided into six Boards, also known as the Boards at the Center, which served the caliph and worked with him to govern the caliphate. These were the *Diwan al-Qudat* (Board of Justice), the *Diwan al-Jund* (Board of Military), the *Diwan al-Kharaj* (Board of Revenue), the *Diwan al-Khatam* (Board of Signet), *Diwan al-Barid* (Board of Posts), and the *Diwan al-Rasa'il* (Board of Correspondence).

**The Sufyanids**

Although Umayyad is the name of the entire caliphate and is often called a dynasty, many of the individual rulers themselves developed their own long-lasting personal dynasties based on hereditary bloodlines. Another important element to note about many of the Islamic caliphates is that each one believed to be of a dynasty or lineage shared with Muhammad. For the Umayyad family, who were also called the Banu Abd-Shams, tradition stated they shared a common ancestor with Muhammad named Abd Manaf ibn Qusai who came from Mecca. While Muhammad was descended from Abd Manaf's son Hashim, the Umayyads were of a different son, Abd-Shams. Both families were considered separate clans because of the traditional rules of patriarchal lineage, but of the same tribe, the Quraish.

Tradition dictated the Umayyads hated the Hashemites before the birth of Muhammad, and the deep animosity only worsened followed the Battle of Badr in 624. During the battle, three prominent leaders of the Umayyad clan were murdered in a three-on-three melee with leaders of the Hashemites. Legend states the leaders were Utbah ibn Rabi'ah, Walid ibn Utbah and Shaybah for the Umayyads and Ali, Hamza ibn Abdul-Muttalib and Ubaydah ibn al-Harith for the Hashemites.[19]

Despite the growing number of opponents, Abu Sufyan continued his mission to exterminate the growing number of Muslims in the region. He waged another battle in an attempt to curb the power of the Muslims of Medina and take revenge for the defeat at Badr. This second armed conflict became known as the Battle of Uhud and occurred throughout March 625. Abu Sufyan led his army of Qurayshi Meccans against the forces of Muhammad in Medina.

While the Meccans struggled to gain ground at Badr, Uhud was considered a success because the Muslims incurred greater losses than the Meccans despite having the home advantage. Islamic tradition often seeks to emphasize the supposed barbaric quality of the Meccans during the battle by including anecdotes about individual brutalities. One of the most well-known stories is that Abu Sufyan's wife, a woman named Hind, climbed on the battlefield and cut open the corpse of Hamza, a rival. She then removed his liver and tried to eat it. There is no historical

---

[19] Giorgio Levi Della Vida, "Umayya b. Abd Shams" ikn Bearman, P. J.; Bianquis, Th.; Bosworth, C. E.; van Donzel, E. & Heinrichs, W. P. (eds.). *The Encyclopaedia of Islam, New Edition, Volume X: T–U*. Leiden: E. J. Brill, 2000, p. 838.

reference for whether or not corpse desecration was common practice during these early struggles.

Unfortunately for the Meccans, their power would not last. In 629 , less than five years after the initial success in Mecca, Muhammad beat back Abu Sufyan and took control of the city. He announced general amnesty, at which point Abu Sufyan, Hind, and the rest of the family converted to Islam. Sources indicate their son would become the future caliph Muawiyah I. However, the Umayyads would not ascend to power until Uthman ibn Affan became the third caliph. Uthman ibn Affan was an early companion of Muhammad as well as being his son-in-law and second cousin.

As caliph, Uthman ruled from 644-656 but failed to establish a dynasty. Instead of passing down power to his sons, he chose to appoint members of his familial clan to notable positions of power in the region, including his first cousin Marwan ibn al-Hakam.[20] Marwan became the top advisor to the caliph, which drew the ire of the Hashemite companions of Muhammad. According to sources, Marwan and his father Al-Hakam ibn Abi al-As had both been exiled from Medina by Muhammad himself. The Hashemites were further angered at the promotion of Walid ibn Uqba, Marwan's half-brother, as governor of Kufa. Walid ibn Uqba was a notable drinker and was accused of leading prayer while under the influence. Finally, Abdullah ibn Saad became the governor of Egypt despite his lack of experience, replacing the more favored Amr ibn al-As.[21]

Besides these slights to the Hashemite clan, Caliph Uthman further chose to consolidate Muawiyah's governorship of Syria and granted him control over more territory. While Muawiyah proved to be a capable and successful leader, the Hashemites still resented Uthman's position. Muawiyah, meanwhile, would go on to develop one of the most disciplined armies on the continent, composed primarily of nearby Syrian Arabs. Over time, Uthman came to trust and rely upon Muawiyah more and more, eventually appointing him as the governor of Syria when the previous leader succumbed to a plague that killed 25,000 people.[22] By 649, Muawiyah chose to expand his power base and created a navy led by Christian sailors and Muslim troops. This navy proved capable and managed to defeat the Byzantine navy in 655, resulting in the opening of the Mediterranean Sea to trade and conquest. This opening would prove beneficial to later iterations of the Umayyads who sought to gain power in the region.[23]

While Uthman was caliph, he chose to relax many of the restrictions placed by his predecessor, Umar ibn Al-Khattab. Former caliph Umar ibn Al-Khattab (sometimes written as Omar with the title "Al-Farooq"), was one of the most pious and just rulers of the Umayyad Caliphate. He was an expert Muslim jurist and also one of the most powerful Muslim rulers in history. While he

---

[20] G. R. Hawting, *The First Dynasty of Islam: The Umayyad Caliphate AD 661–750 (2nd Edition)*, London and New York: Routledge, 2000.

[21] Ibid.

[22] Fred M. Donner, *The Early Islamic Conquests*, Princeton: Princeton University Press, 1981.

[23] Donner, *The Early Islamic Conquests,* 83-84.

held the throne, he enacted numerous policies designed to control the morals of his people, particularly administrators. He reformed the code of law, removed Christians and Jews from holy territory in Africa, and commanded his subordinates to control any vices they may have, including full abstinence of alcohol and full recognition of holy days.

Caliph Umar ibn Al-Khattab also implemented several other influential policies. If he believed any of his governors or commanders was becoming greedy, lustful, or power hungry, then the official was stripped of his position. Likewise, armies were forced to stay in encampments away from cities that were under attack. This way, Umar ibn Al-Khattab believed the soldiers and commanders would not be tempted to loot and pillage and would not turn away from the teachings of Allah. When Uthman came to power, he was more lenient with his governors.

Besides working with his administrators and allowing them to live more relaxed lives, Uthman also needed to deal with growing tensions between the different tribes of the Arab population. Although these differences had been discouraged while Muhammad was alive, they resurfaced over territorial disputes and claims to power. Iraq and Syria were most notable for issues, and the local Sassanid Empire continued to wage war against nearby Byzantium. Uthman's decisions ultimately led to his murder in 656 at the hands of an unknown assassin.

The next individual to rise to the position of caliph in the burgeoning Umayyad dynasty was a man known to history as Ali. Ali was the cousin and son-in-law of Muhammad – indicating he married his cousin's daughter. Once he took power, Ali switched the location of the capital from Medina to Kufa, which irritated a broad range of factions in the region. As noted earlier, Ali experienced initial success against the supporters of Aisha at the Battle of the Camel in 656, but he ran into trouble a year later (July 657) against Muawiyah.

For Muawiyah, his dynasty was the Sufyanids or "descendants of Abu Sufyan." They would reign from 661-684 and would only have three rulers: Muawiyah, his son, and his grandson. While Muawiyah ruled, the kingdom managed to maintain internal security while being able to expand externally. Only one major rebellion occurred when Huir ibn 'Adi al-Kindi of Kufa, a former companion of Muhammad, supported the descendants of Ali. His movement was rapidly suppressed, however, by the governor of Iraq.

To maintain internal peace and stability, Muawiyah encouraged peaceful coexistence between Muslims and religious minorities like the Christians of Syria. Historians note the caliph's rule as being one of the only reigns characterized by "peace and prosperity for Christians and Arabs alike," and Muawiyah even employed Syrian Christians as advisors to the court.[24] At the same time, the Umayyad caliphate launched an aggressive and unceasing war against the nearby Byzantine Roman Empire for territory and resources.

---

[24] Kennedy, *The Prophet and the Age of the Caliphates*, p. 76.

Through superior numbers and tactics, the caliphate claimed Rhodes and Crete and assaulted the city of Constantinople itself. Ultimately, however, that assault was a failure and spawned a largescale Christian uprising by the Mardaites. The Mardaites were a group of early Christians who lived in the Nur Mountains. As the Umayyad caliphate and other Muslim groups sought to claim the region, the Mardaites adopted an aggressive fighting style and sided with the Byzantine Empire to push the invaders back. Their numbers swelled through the arrival of thousands of runaway slaves from Muslim territory, resulting in an ethnically diverse society and fighting force. The Mardaites were so deadly in combat that Muslim resources from the time refer to the fighters as being "sick" or "insane."[25] Through their presence, the Byzantine Empire managed to retain a hold on the Nur Mountains and even forced Muawiyah to pay tribute as part of a short-lived peace treaty.

The first Sufyanid caliph was not done with Asia. Over the next decade, Muawiyah would target Kabul, Bukhara, and Samarkand, leading to their conquest. All three would become a part of the growing Islamic empire of the 7th century. At the same time, when he wasn't trying to break further into Asia and Europe, Muawiyah focused on Africa. He was responsible for overseeing a large-scale military expansion throughout North Africa, which would be the foundation of Kairouan. Kairouan, sometimes spelled Qayrawan, was a significant center of early Sunni scholarship and education. It currently serves as the capital of Tunisia and played an important role in the Umayyad power structure in North Africa.

Eventually, Muawiyah fell ill and passed away. Yazid I, the eldest son of Muawiyah, rose to the throne and was crowned in 680, but his rule did not go unchallenged. Numerous prominent Muslims opposed the idea of hereditary succession, including Abd-Allah ibn al-Zubayr. Abd-Allah ibn al-Zubayr was the son of one of the original companions of Muhammad. Standing with him was Husayn ibn Ali, a younger son of the original Ali who opposed Muawiyah.

The challenge and ensuing conflict became known as the Second Fitna. During this civil war, Ibn al-Zubayr was forced to flee Medina for Mecca because of his political views. He remained there in opposition and exile until his death, unable to dislodge Yazid I from the throne. At the same time, Husayn was also forced to flee, unable to muster the forces necessary to combat the military of the Umayyad Caliphate. The people of Kufa invited him to lodge in the city, but Husayn and his family were intercepted, captured, and executed on their way during the Battle of Karbala. Yazid I sent his victorious soldiers to occupy Kufa and quash the rebellious spirit of the city.

However, Yazid I's victory was not complete. Once word of Husayn's death spread, opposition throughout the caliphate grew. Multiple movements and rebellions rose, especially when the Kharijites heard word of the unrest. Two central movements emerged with one centered in Medina and another in Basra. Yazid I was forced to invest his time and energy into suppressing

---

[25] Christos G. Makrypoulias, "Mardaites in Asia Minor," *Encyclopedia of the Hellenic World - Asia Minor*, 2005.

the growing unrest. In 683, he sent his army to confront the rebels of Medina at the Battle of al-Harra. Once they defeated their initial opponent, the army then went on to besiege Mecca. The soldiers pillaged the city and damaged several influential cultural centers, including the Grand Mosque of Medina and the Kaaba in nearby Mecca. Resentment among the people grew as they saw their heritage and religious centers attacked.

News traveled slowly through the Umayyad Caliphate, and before the army had broken into Medina and finished the siege of Mecca, Yazid I perished. Once word reached the generals, the Umayyad army was ordered to return to Damascus. Ibn al-Zubayr took control of Mecca while Yazid's son, Muawiyah II, took the throne, but few recognized his rule outside of Syria. Instead, two factions developed: the Confederation of Qays and the Quda'a. The Confederation supported Ibn al-Zubayr while the Quda'a recognized Marwan, a descendant of Umayya through the bloodline of Wa'il ibn Umayyah.[26] Both forces went to war, and the supporters of Marwan triumphed at the Battle of Marj Rahit, ensuring Marwan became caliph in 684.

### The Marwanids

The line of succession begun by Marwan would become known as the Marwanids. The new caliph's first task upon ascending to the throne was to assert his authority and stymy the rival claims of Ibn al-Zubayr. Ibn al-Zubayr had a much greater base of support and was recognized as the caliph throughout the majority of the Islamic world. Marwan's solution was to retake the regions which supported Ibn al-Zubayr, beginning with Egypt. He succeeded in capturing the territory, but he died in 685, so his rule lasted a scant nine months.

Marwan's eldest son, Abd al-Malik, then became caliph. His early rule was marred by the revolt of Al-Mukhtar. Al-Mukhtar, full name Al-Mukhtar ibn Abi Ubayd Al-Thaqafi, a revolutionary in Kufa who supported the rule of the lineage of Ali. His goal was to promote Muhammad ibn al-Hanafiyyah, one of the sons of the deceased Ali, to the throne. Somewhat surprisingly, Ibn al-Hanafiyyah is believed to have had no connection to the revolt on his behalf and made no claims to the caliphate.

Al-Mukhtar commanded his troops to stop the armies of Abd al-Malik from reclaiming territory throughout Africa on behalf of the Umayyad Caliphate, and they engaged in multiple battles over the next year, but al-Mukhtar gained little ground. Although his armies defeated the Umayyads in battle near the Khazir River near Mosul in 686, al-Mukhtar and his revolutionaries were crushed the next year. With less opposition, the Umayyad troops managed to reconquer Iraq and marched upon the forces of Ibn al-Zubayr, who remained a threat until 692. In that year, Ibn al-Zubayr was defeated during an attack on Mecca.

---

[26] According to historic lineage, Marwan was the cousin of Muawiyah I. The battle for the caliphate was fought between a series of supporters and detractors of Muhammad and a select few families and clans who sought leadership amongst themselves.

Once he consolidated his power, Abd al-Malik turned to domestic policies and improvements. Chief among these was the construction of the Dome of the Rock in Jerusalem, which would be completed in 692. Because it was being built during the conflict with Ibn al-Zubayr, numerous historians believe the Dome of the Rock was intended to rival the Kaaba as a destination for dedicated pilgrims. At the same time, Abd al-Malik centralized the administration of the caliphate and established Arabic as the official language of government and business. He would then become the first creator of a distinct Muslim currency designed to replace the Byzantine and Sasanian coins used in the past.

**A late 7th century Umayyad coin**

**An Umayyad coin weight**

Later in his rule, Abd al-Malik adopted an aggressive foreign policy against Byzantium. He recommended his predecessors' offensive warfare and marched upon Byzantine territory in 692, breaking the peace that had existed between the two powers since 680. The first major success for the Umayyads was the Battle of Sebastopolis, during which Byzantine leader Leontios led an army of 30,000 Slavs against the Muslim soldiers. Unfortunately for him, 20,000 Slavs defected during the conflict, resulting in a massive loss for Byzantium. Caliph Abd al-Malik thus reestablished control over Armenia and Caucasian Iberia and developed a more positive relationship with the native population of the region.[27]

Abd al-Malik remained an effective ruler until his death in 705. At this point, his son, Al-Walid I, became caliph. Although Al-Walid was an active builder and ruler, sponsoring the construction of both the Al-Masjid al-Nabawi and the Great Mosque of Damascus, he did not remain in power for long. That said, despite the fact he only ruled until 715, he gained several influential regions, particularly the Sindh and Punjab regions of the Indus River. Following the death of his best general, Muhammad bin Qasim, Al-Walid I retired from the project of conquering India and

---

[27] John F. Haldon, *Byzantium in the 7th century*, (Cambridge University Press, 1997), 72.

instead turned his remaining months in power to domestic pursuits. To protect his claims in the region of Iraq, he requested the Umayyad governor of the region to import additional Syrian troops.

When Al-Walid died in 715, he was replaced by his younger brother Sulayman. Sulayman was one of the least effective leaders of the Umayyad Caliphate, ruling for a scant two years. He is best known for his protracted siege of Constantinople, which resulted in a serious failure that ended serious expansionist ambitions against the Byzantine capital and the northern extents of the empire.

Another major defeat for Sulayman was against the Chinese Tang dynasty. The Umayyad Caliphate drew Chinese ire when they deposed the ikhshid of the Principality of Farghana and replaced him with a new ruler.[28] The deposed ikhshid fled to nearby Kucha and requested Chinese intervention to protect his sovereignty as well as that of the Tangs. Unwilling to allow Islamic influence to spread further into Asia, the Chinese sent General Zhang Xiaosong with 10,000 troops to Farghana.

Zhang Xiaosong routed the invading Umayyads and restored the ikhshid to power. However, the Umayyads were not done. In 717, they attacked Transoxiana in an attempt to thwart the Chinese military garrisons' hold in the region. The goal was to claim the Four Garrisons of Anxi district. The ensuing conflict was the Battle of Aksu, during which Umayyad commander Al-Yasukuni was forced to flee to Tashkent.[29] This was the final humiliating defeat for Sulayman.

Later that year, Sulayman's cousin Umar ibn Abd al-Aziz would become caliph. He became the only Umayyad caliph to be considered a genuine caliph or *khalifa* rather than just a worldly king, or *malik*. Umar became well-known and honored for his decision to tackle the fiscal problems associated with religious conversion to Islam. This was essential as the majority of the people living within the borders of the Umayyad Caliphate were not Muslim. Instead, they were Christian, Jewish, Zoroastrian, or members of smaller cults, religions, and ethnic groups.

As non-Muslims, the majority of the population was required to pay the *jizyah*, or a religious tax. This created a major problem for the administration as widespread popular conversion to Islam would be unprofitable and diminish state revenues. Regional and provincial governors thus actively discouraged individuals from converting. Umar's exact actions towards resolution are unknown. Historical sources indicate he proposed similar treatment for Arab and non-Arab Muslims at a time when Arab Muslims were treated as superior to converts from different ethnic backgrounds. He also eliminated several of the obstacles that prevented non-Arab conversion. Sources indicate this could mean removing troublesome provincial governors in favor of more devout or progressive administrators.

---

[28] The proper term Ikhshid was the title for the Iranian rulers of the region in the pre-Islamic and Early Islamic periods.

[29] Haldon, *Byzantium in the 7th century.*

Umar was one of the most influential leaders of the Umayyad Caliphate despite his short reign. He died in 720, a scant three years after his coronation. Without a direct heir, he would be succeeded by another son of Abd al-Malik, Yazid II. Yazid proved to be an unpopular caliph best known for his declaration of an iconoclastic edict that targeted Christian imagery. He ordered all Christian images destroyed throughout Umayyad territory, spawning civil unrest. Iraq revolted once again; this time led by rival Yazid ibn al-Muhallab. It was quickly quashed and Yazid II would only rule until his death in 724.

The last son of former ruler Abd al-Malik became caliph following Yazid II's demise. This son, Hisham, possessed the longest and most eventful rule out of all of his siblings. One of his first actions was to move the official court closer to the Byzantine border. The chosen location was Resafa in norther Syria. From Resafa, Hisham could resume hostilities with the Byzantine Empire. It was the first major action against the Byzantines since the failed siege of Constantinople. Instead of beginning with direct confrontation, Hashim ordered his troops to conduct short military campaigns and raids into Anatolia. Unfortunately, the Byzantine Empire responded by sending their own armies. At the Battle of Akroinon, the Umayyads suffered a major defeat and were unable to gain any new territory.

It was at this point in the caliphate's history that the Umayyads turned towards Europe. Using bases in North and Western Africa, the caliphs ordered their generals to collect willing converts from the Berbers and raid the coastal towns owned by the Visigoths. The Visigothic Christian kingdoms were spread out across the Iberian Peninsula – the location of modern Spain and Portugal. Permanent occupation by the Umayyads began as early as 711 and would continue northward into southeastern Gaul.

While expansion began under Al-Walid I, it would end with Hisham. In 732, the Arab army, bolstered by Berber soldiers, failed to defeat the Franks at the Battle of Tours. The Franks were a prominent combination of European ethnic groups populating the region of modern France, Belgium, and western Germany. They were often at odds with the neighboring Gauls, a Celtic people that had expanded into the region of Switzerland, Luxembourg, and part of France. Unfortunately for the Arabs, the Franks possessed a moderately centralized empire with a standing military that refused to back down in the face of enemy expansion.

The loss at the Battle of Tours would not be the most severe military defeat under the rule of Hisham. Seven years later, in 739, a major Berber revolt occurred in North Africa. Throughout the Umayyad Caliphate's expansion, the Berbers had formed the brunt of the military force, but even though the native western Africans had converted to Islam in large numbers, they were treated as second class citizens to Arabs. They did not receive recognition for their accomplishments, were not promoted like Arab soldiers, and often formed segregated regiments assigned to the worst tasks. The Berbers were no longer willing to accept Umayyad rule. Many of the soldiers stationed in Iberia rebelled and left their posts, shaking the power of the caliphate.

From the rebellion came some of the first Muslim states to exist outside of the caliphate, including Morocco.

Without the backing of the Berbers, Umayyad influence in Iberia dwindled. The Visigoth Christian kingdoms worked together to eliminate the Umayyad armies holding al-Andalus and pushed the caliphate back. By the middle of the 8th century, the Umayyads claimed only southern Iberia, while the Visigoths held strong in the north. At the same time, the Arab military began to crumble across the empire. In India, for example, the south Indian Chalukya dynasty defeated the encroaching Umayyad army while the north Indian Pratiharas dynasty did the same.[30]

These losses were the greatest of Hisham's career, but they were far from the only ones. In the 730s, the Umayyad Caliphate attempted to displace the Khazars and head into Eastern Europe, but they were soundly defeated at the Battle of Marj Ardabil. Even when the generals launched a massive invasion all the way to the Volga River, the Khazars remained undefeated, and the Umayyads were forced to limit their hopes for a northern expansion. Before this, Hisham had attempted to move east and subdue Tokharistan and Transoxiana, but the invasions failed miserably and increased the discontent of religious minorities who had been promised tax relief if they chose to convert to Islam. Revolts broke out throughout the empire.

The issue of taxation against religious minorities, as well as that of rights for non-Arab Muslims, continued to be the source of major problems in the Umayyad Caliphate. Further compounding these difficulties was the issue of succession, which had not been settled. Political rivals still vied for power, each with a claim of either religious superiority or a close tie to the Islamic prophet Muhammad. The poor rule of Hisham was the straw that broke the camel's back for various rebels and rivals throughout the empire, leading to the Third Fitna in 744.

The Third Fitna was yet another series of civil wars and political uprisings against not only the Marwanid line, but the Umayyad Caliphate as a whole. It began with the death of Hisham in 743. According to a decree by Yazid II, Hisham's successor was to be his brother al-Walid II. At first, the people seemed willing to accept their new caliph. Hisham had been unpopular and al-Walid II's first act upon coming to power was to increase military pay in attempt to appease the soldiers. However, he was also a man who desired earthly pleasures over spiritual enlightenment and religious devotion. He avoided his spiritual duties in favor of amassing more wealth and decorating his "desert palaces" like Qusayr Amra and Khirbat al- Mafjar.[31]

For many of his political rivals, al-Walid II's failure to uphold the fundamental tenets of Islam served only to breed resentment. Even within the Umayyad family itself, al-Walid II proved to be unpopular. Instead of appointing one of his numerous male cousins as his successor, the

[30] B. A. Litvinsky; A. H. Jalilov; A. I. Kolesnikov. "The Arab Conquest." In B.A. Litvinsky. (ed.). *History of civilizations of Central Asia, Volume III: The crossroads of civilizations: A.D. 250 to 750*, (Paris: UNESCO Publishing, 1996).
[31] Hawting, *The First Dynasty of Islam*.

caliph instead chose his two underage sons. When the family protested, al-Walid II ordered the flogging, imprisonment, and torture of his cousin, Sulayman ibn Hisham.[32] Further opposition on a large scale grew when al-Walid II persecuted the Qadariyya sect, a group of early Islamic theologians who assigned humans free will and absolved God of all evil in the world. He then became involved in the rivalries of the northern and southern Arab tribes, breeding resentment from all four factions involved in the disputes.

Tensions reached their peak in April 744, when Yazid III marched into Damascus. Yazid III was one of the sons of al-Walid I and possessed a claim to the Umayyad throne. His supporters, who had bolstered their ranks with Kalbis from the surrounding area, overthrew the guards and seized the town. Yazid III was declared the new caliph. Al-Walid II, who had been vacationing at one of his desert palaces, fled the region and arrived at al-Bakhra near Palmyra. He garnered little support from the local Kalbis and Qaysis, but managed to muster a small force. However, the majority fled when Yazid III's army arrived. Without protection, al-Walid II was captured, executed, and had his severed head sent as a trophy to Damascus. A local pro-Qaysi uprising then tried to march upon Damascus in an attempt to place the Sufyanid Abu Muhammad al-Sufyani on the throne, but it was easily defeated. Abu Muhammad found himself in prison alongside al-Walid II's sons.

Although he took the throne by force and only served for a brief period, Yazid III proved to be an exemplary caliph and one of the most efficient rulers the Umayyad Caliphate enjoyed. He modeled himself after the pious Umar II and earned the esteem and favor of the religious administrators who had denounced al-Walid II. He further supported the Qadariyya and worked to disassociate his reign from the autocratic tendencies of his predecessors by avoiding the excesses and abuses that drew ire in the past. This meant reducing taxes rather than increasing them, bringing soldiers home instead of sending them on long expansionist wars, not enriching the Umayyads and their family members and adherents, and not giving preference to the region of Syria. In other words, he wanted to create a fairer caliphate that focused less on the enrichment and glorification of the Umayyads and more on developing a focused, pious, and centralized empire.

Yazid III further distinguished himself by claiming the community chose him and therefore possessed the right to depose him if they were not pleased with his practices.[33] None of the previous Umayyad rulers could host such a claim or even incorporated the broad public – or at the least the influential men – in such a way. While this could have been a turning point for the autocratic rule of the Umayyad Caliphate, Yazid III was the first and last leader for several centuries to even attempt to incorporate broader public appeal into his tenets of rule.

Although he was successful, Yazid III did not live long. He died after only six months and left

---

[32] Ibid.
[33] Hawting, *The First Dynasty of Islam*, p. 95.

a power vacuum in his place. The figure who would emerge from the void was Marwan II. Marwan II supervised many of the campaigns against the Byzantine Empire and the native Khazars for many years. When he learned about the death of al-Walid II, he originally planned to claim the caliphate for himself. However, he was forced to put down a Kalbi rebellion instead. When Yazid III came to power, Marwan II was sent to Upper Mesopotamia and resided in Harran.

When Yazid III died, Marwan II saw his opportunity to become the new caliph. He gathered his forces and marched into Syria. To bolster his public support, Marwan II claimed to be fighting on the behalf of the imprisoned sons of al-Walid II. As their champion, he gathered numerous followers from the local Qaysis and Hims of the region and marched unopposed until he traveled between Baalbek and Damascus. There, he discovered another experienced general, Sulayman ibn Hisham, waiting for him. Sulayman headed the Dhakwaniyya private army and received support from the regional Kalbis. He attempted to prevent the advancement of Marwan II, but suffered a brutal loss and fled to Damascus to avoid being captured. Those he left behind were forced to pledge allegiance to the sons of al-Walid II before being executed by their compatriots for disloyalty to Sulayman.[34]

Without the imminent opposition of Sulayman, Marwan II entered the capital of Damascus in peace in December. Upon reaching the palace, he was declared caliph. To avoid reprisals and maintain peace throughout the region, Marwan II encouraged the administrative districts in Syria to choose their own governors and officials rather than picking them himself. This way, local rebels were able to exert some form of control over who possessed power. This decision reduced support for Marwan II's opponents, and Sulayman ibn Hisham eventually arrived in Damascus to submit.

Unfortunately, while Marwan II demonstrated some political savvy in the beginning of his reign, he quickly made the poor decision to move the capital of the caliphate from Damascus to Harran, effectively leaving Syria. According to historians, "[f]or the first time a caliph seemed to have abandoned Syria altogether."[35] It is important to note at this point that Damascus and Syria in general had been chosen as the capital for the Umayyads to control the underlying waves of rebellion and resentment existing in the region. By leaving, Marwan II fueled mistrust in his leadership and left a simmering population with the explosive potential of a powder keg. Almost immediately after his departure, Marwan II faced trouble in the form of a Kalbi revolt in Palestine in the summer of 745. He was forced to return to Syria and put down the revolt city by city, overthrowing and killing many of the local governors and leaders who strove to liberate the region from the larger control of the Umayyads.

At this point, Marwan II realized he needed to reaffirm his hold on the caliphate. With Syria in

---

[34] Hawting, *The First Dynasty of Islam,* p. 97.
[35] M.A. Shaban, *The Abbasid Revolution,* (Cambridge: Cambridge University Press, 1979).

his clutches, Marwan II ordered the other living members of the Umayyad dynasty to converge upon his palace and bear witness as he named his sons as his heirs in a hereditary line of succession. He then assembled a new army to send to Iraq to put down the revolts popping up throughout the territory. Yet again, he was unfortunate. As soon as the army reached Rusafa, it mutinied and instead accepted Sulayman ibn Hisham as the true leader of the caliphate. The army marched upon and took nearby Qinnasrin where it was joined by a mass of local rebels.

With the majority of his army defeated, Sulayman ibn Hisham was forced to once more escape, this time heading to Palmyra. Once there, he gathered some supplies and moved to Kufa. The surviving portion of his army did not join him. Instead, it withdrew to Hims, where Sulayman's brother took command. The brother, Sa'id, took too long to recuperate and collect his forces; Marwan arrived before Hims was prepared and besieged the city.

Throughout the winter of 745 and 746, Marwan attacked the city walls and wore down the remaining supporters of Sulayman. With supplies low, the army at Hims was forced to capitulate. With the opposing forces once more subdued, Marwan refused to show any more leniency to the Syrians. At this point, the Syrians had rebelled multiple times, forged an army, and destroyed many of the caliphate's resources in an attempt to change the line of succession. To reduce further rebellion, Marwan went between the Syrian towns, destroying the walls so they were unprotected. According to historical sources, some of the affected cities included Damascus and Jerusalem.

### The Abbasid Revolution

Marwan's troubles were not limited to Syria. He faced significant opposition in Egypt and Iraq, where local governors attempted to restore the preeminence of their regions in the power of the Umayyad Caliphate. Although Marwan was able to suppress the rebellions and regain a semblance of control over the territories, his tribulations were not over. On the horizon loomed the Abbasid Revolution.

The Abbasid Revolution had its origins in 719, the year missionaries began to seek support in Khurasan for "a member of the House of the Prophet who shall be pleasing to everyone."[36] On the surface, the mission sounded like basic proselytism and the spreading of Islam. However, the missionaries were actually attempting to drum up support for the Abbasids. The Umayyad Caliphate was growing increasingly unpopular among the different Muslim sects, and the Abbasids began to receive support from Arabs and non-Arabs alike.[37] Non-Arabs were perhaps the most influential, as large numbers of Christians, Jews, and Zoroastrians were dissatisfied with their sociopolitical limitations in the current caliphate.

The Abbasids were descendants of Abbas ibn Abd al-Muttalib, one of the youngest uncles of

---

[36] Ira M. Lapidus, *A History of Islamic Societies*, (Cambridge: Cambridge University Press, 2002), p. 58.
[37] John Esposito (Ed.), *The Oxford History of Islam,* (Oxford: Oxford University Press, 1999).

Muhammad and a member of the same familial clan. They claimed to be the true successors of the prophet Muhammad and manipulated the tense political situation in the Umayyad Caliphate to bolster their position amongst the people. In addition to drumming up a powerful base among non-Arabs, the Abbasids and their supporters also drew power from discontented Shia Muslims and Sunni non-Arab Muslims who felt their religious views and social position were not respected by the current hereditary dynasty. These ranks were further bolstered by former members of the Shia rebellions that sprang up throughout Syria due to alliances and perceived wrongdoings during the Second and Third Fitnas.[38]

During the first half of the 8th century, Kufa rapidly became a center for opposition to the Umayyad dynasty. Of particular importance in the region were the supporters of Ali and the minority Shias. According to historians of the Islamic caliphates, the well-known Persian general Abu Muslim first met with Abbasid agents in the region around 741. At this point, he made initial overtures to join the opposition of the Umayyads and eventually worked his way to meeting Imam Ibrahim, the leader of the Abbasids, during a trip to Mecca.

Due to his military prowess and charismatic personality, Abu Muslim became the de facto leader of the Hashimiyya in Khurasan by 746. Instead of being an open rebellion against the Umayyads, the Hashimiyya developed an underground resistance movement alongside the Abbasids to slowly enlarge their popular support. Secret communicative networks were mapped out throughout the eastern half of the Umayyad Caliphate, and spies were used to not only drum up support for the Abbasids but also spread dissent and doubt about Umayyad leadership.

Buildup continued through the Zaydi Revolt in Iraq and the Berber Revolts in Iberia and Maghreb, during which the underclasses of the current Islamic caliphate began to rebel against partisan leadership and the Umayyad failure to treat converted Muslims the same as Arab Muslims. The Hashimiyya also remained active but secretive during the Ibadi rebellion in Hijaz and Yemen, the Third Fitna, and the revolt of al-Harith ibn Surayi in Khurasan.

Despite remaining secret, the Abbasids and their allies were highly effective at manipulating local politics and grudges to increase outward rebellion against the Umayyads. The Umayyad Caliphate, meanwhile, was besieged in all four corners of the empire and expended numerous resources attempting to regain control over territory that now stretched over three continents. Some modern historians, including G.R. Hawting, assert the Umayyads were stretched so thin they would have been unable to thwart the Abbasid machinations had they known of them in the first place.[39] Around the Revolt of Ibn Surayi in 746, the Abbasids were ready to make their move.

Ibn Surayj was the leader of a social and religious rebellion against the Umayyads. He began

---

[38] Ibid.
[39] Hala Mundhir Fattah, *A Brief History of Iraq,* (New York: Infobase Publishing, 2009), p. 77.

his initial revolt at Merv but failed to outmaneuver the caliphate's soldiers, resulting in the loss of many civilians and his own secretary and confidante. Eventually, ibn Surayj was able to discover some allies in the region, banding together with nearby rebel factions. Combined, the rebels were able to drive the Umayyad forces back from Merv to Nishapur. Unfortunately, Ibn Surayj was betrayed and lost his forces and by the summer of 747, the Umayyads sued for peace. The rebel victory was short lived though, as one of the sons of ibn Surayj assassinated the backstabbing rebels. Shi'ite revolts broke out throughout the region, and Abu Muslim took advantage of the chaos to launch his own rebellion in June 747.

On June 9, Abu Muslim raised the sign of the Black Standard and initiated an open rebellion against local Umayyad leaders in Merv.[40] At this point, Abu Muslim had over 10,000 soldiers under his control. By February 14, 748, he ousted the Umayyad governor Nasr ibn Sayyar and dispatched part of his army to the west where the soldiers marched upon Qumis. To bolster his ranks, Abu Muslim relied upon the Abbasid officers Qahtaba ibn Shabib al-Ta'i, Al-Hasan ibn Qahtaba, and Humayd ibn Qahtaba. These men, a father and his two sons, were tasked with pursuing ibn Sayyar and continuing to push him west, away from Abu Muslim's revolt.

Al-Ta'i became the most significant officer in the west while Abu Muslim remained in the east. With the aid of his sons, al-Ta'i defeated an Umayyad force of 10,000 at Gorgan in August and then captured the city of Rey where Ibn Sayyar had attempted to regroup with reinforcements. Unfortunately, the city fell and Ibn Sayyar died fleeing west to Hamedan. Al-Ta'i would appear on the scene shortly thereafter and defeat the 50,000 soldiers sent by the Umayyads to Isfahan, weakening the caliphate's power in the west.

The Umayyads' last stand would come at Khorasan. The remaining soldiers were survivors of Hamedan, along with the remnants of Ibn Sayyar's forces. At Nahavand, the military garrisoned and locked themselves in the city,[41] but relief contingents from Syria failed to arrive as Qahtaba cut them off. While his son laid siege to the Umayyad forces in Nahavand, Qahtaba cut a deal with the captured troops. The Syrian contingent pledged loyalty to the Abbasids and shared military secrets, resulting in the systematic execution of the Umayyad soldiers left in Khorasan. Umayyad power in the region crumbled, ending a ninety-year reign.

Around this time, Abu Muslim strengthened Abbasid control over the Muslim far east by facilitating more rebellions. The Abbasid rulers took advantage of their newfound power to appoint loyal governors in Bactria and Transoxiana. Anyone who could oppose their control was offered a peace deal, only to be double crossed and destroyed once they accepted and laid down their weapons.[42]

Once Khorasan was under their control, the Abbasids made a rapid transition into

---

[40] Richard N. Frye (Ed.), *The Cambridge History of Iran*, (Cambridge: Cambridge University Press, 1977).
[41] Matthew Gordon, *The Rise of Islam*, (Hackett Publishing Company, 2005).
[42] Ibid.

Mesopotamia. This region was one of the oldest and most coveted of the Umayyad holdings and was necessary to exert total power over the Muslim world. In August 749, Umayyad commander Yazid ibn Umar al-Fazari tried to intercept Abbasid al-Ta'i before he reached the city of Kufa. Before he could make it, a separate Abbasid military group raided al-Fazari's encampment. Al-Ta'i's forces took part, but the commander himself would perish in battle.

Losing men and supplies fast, al-Fazari was forced to flee to the nearby city of Wasit. His soldiers reinforced the garrisons and managed to resist the Siege of Wasit from August 749 until July of 750. The Abbasids viewed al-Fazari's position in the city as beneficial to their own aims. The usurpers were able to leave a small number of soldiers around the area to besiege Wasit, and the rest of the army was available to go on the offensive and attack the other Umayyad holdings.[43]

While Wasit was under siege, the Abbasids crossed the Euphrates River and marched on Kufa. Inside the city's walls, the son of a disgraced Umayyad official started a pro-Abbasid riot in the citadel. Sources agree the son acted to avenge his father's torture and execution at the hands of the Umayyads. When the Abbasid commander al-Hasan bin Qahtaba arrived in September of 749, he was able to walk through the gates and take Kufa with few casualties.

Once in Kufa, the Abbasids faced a minor challenge from one of their officers, Abu Salama. Abu Salama's connection to the Abbasids was tenuous, and he supported them mainly because of their financial backing. While in the city, he tried to drum up support for a rival Alid leader. One of his confidantes reported these actions to the Abbasids, and they responded rapidly. After a brief consensus, they anointed As-Saffah as the new caliph of Kufa and held an official ceremony at the mosque. As-Saffah was the great grandson of al-Abbas, the uncle of Muhammad. Abu Salama pledged his loyalty alongside twelve other military commanders to avoid embarrassment and the repercussions of his political leanings.[44]

While General Qahtaba was busy in Kufa, the Abbasids sent the combined forces of two more commanders, Abdallah ibn Ali and Abu Awn Abd al-Malik ibn Yazid, to broader Mesopotamia. Because the armies were approaching from different directions, they arranged to meet on the left bank of the Tigris River where they attacked Umayyad forces. This battle became known as the Battle of the Zab. Marwan II, the current caliph of the Umayyads, saw his army completely destroyed and after nine days on the field, he was forced to turn tale and flee, sealing the fate of the Umayyads. As Marwan II made his way through Syria and to Egypt, the Abbasid armies snapped up the Umayyad towns in quick succession.[45]

Eventually, Damascus fell in April 750. Marwan II and his family managed to flee the city but were tracked down in August and brought to Egypt by a small group of loyal soldiers. Historians debate what happened to all of the members of the family. Some claim every individual was

---

[43] Hawting, *The First Dynasty of Islam*, p. 116-117.
[44] Ibid.
[45] Ibid.

executed in Egypt, while some suggest a few of the younger women were allowed to live. Whatever the case may be, the Umayyad dynasty was over. Over the next few months, the final Umayyad military commanders were tracked. Although several were promised amnesty if they surrendered, all of them were executed instead.

The supporters of the Abbasids were from a variety of backgrounds and included almost every level of society, including full Arab Muslims, non-Arab Muslims, and dhimmis. There was also significant military backing, and many of the soldiers were Muslims of non-Arab descent who were tired of Umayyad authority and the caliphate's refusal to acknowledge them as equals to their Arab counterparts. Another common issue was the Umayyad decision to centralize authority and administration in regions where the ethnic peoples were accustomed to a nomadic lifestyle. Non-Muslim subjects revolted against religious discrimination. Although the Abbasids did not promise any changes to the Umayyad administration, many individuals thought someone new holding the reigns of the caliphate would bring necessary reform.[46]

To fully understand the causes of the Abbasid Revolution, it's important to examine the different demographics. Each one experienced varying levels of discontent, but also importantly had different amounts of power. Perhaps the most important were the Shia Muslims who felt the Umayyads did not respect their religious beliefs. Dissent continued to rise and reach a boiling point following the Battle of Karbala in 680. In the Battle of Karbala, the grandson of Muhammad – Husayn ibn Ali – was massacred alongside his family and friends. This event became the rallying cry of the Shias against the Umayyads, and the Abbasids manipulated the memory of Karbala to gain support among the Shia Muslims.[47]

However, although there was general discontent among the Shia Muslims, it would be the Hashimiyya movement that rallied Arab Muslims against the Umayyad dynasty. The original goal, as mentioned earlier, was to replace the Umayyads with a ruling family. The revolts of the Shias actually closely resembled the Shi'ite revolts and uprisings in the past, being centered in cities and led by more influential members of Arab society. However, the Hashimiyya was clear about their desire for an Alid ruler for the caliphate. As the revolts worsened and significant Shia commanders and leaders started to die in battle with the Umayyads, anti-Umayyad sentiment continued to grow. Even better for them, the Shi'ite oppositional leaders were captured and murdered by the Umayyads, leaving the Abbasids as the only realistic alternative to the Umayyads.[48]

Although the Abbasids did not want an Alid ruler, they kept quiet about their true loyalty. Instead, when meeting with other dissidents, they stated they wanted a ruler who was a descendant of Muhammad that the Muslim community would all approve of. Many of the Shi'ite

---

[46] Hawting, *The First Dynasty of Islam*, p. 106.
[47] Ibid.
[48] Gordon, *The Rise of Islam*, p. 46.

Muslims assumed this meant an Alid would ascend to the role of the caliph, and the Abbasids tacitly approved.[49] As time went on, more and more individual groups began to support the Abbasids, partially because they believed the Abbasids were the only group to have enough power to combat the Umayyads. Among their followers were the former supporters of revolutionary leader Mukhtar al-Thaqafi and many of the Kaysanite Shia.

Perhaps the second most influential group of supporters for the Abbasids were non-Arab Sunni Muslims. Many of these individuals converted during the period of the Umayyad conquest. They had been promised the same rights as their Arab counterparts upon conversion, but were treated as second class citizens under the Umayyad regime. In fact, the Umayyad state continues to be well remembered as an Arab-centric state that showed favored status to ethnic Arabs above all else.[50] As an example of how unfair the situation was, Arab Muslims dominated the bureaucracy and held almost all significant military positions. If Arab Muslims chose to live outside of Arabia proper, they were housed in special garrisoned fortresses that became cities within cities. Non-Arab Muslims, often called Mawali, could not live there. There were also strict rules about racially mixed marriages – Arab men could marry non-Arab women, but non-Arab men could not marry Arab women out of cultural concerns for purity.

Surprisingly, while non-Arab Muslims were a powerful group, they only made up 10% of the Umayyad population. The majority were non-Arab non-Muslims who had their territory conquered. However, it was not long before non-Arab Muslims began to outnumber the Arab Muslims, which terrified the Umayyad nobility. Of major concern was that converts would no longer pay the jizya tax stipulated by the Qur'an for non-Muslims. There was a legitimate fear the empire would go bankrupt and no longer be able to remain in control over such an expansive territory. Another issue was cultural. Islam was seen as property of the Arab aristocracy, and if they could not control it, then they would lose some of the sociopolitical power. Since the Umayyads denied equal rights to them, the non-Arab Muslims were happy to side with the Abbasids to gain more power.

Another major cause was the repression of Iranian culture. The Muslim conquest of Persia had disrupted an empire and toppled a powerful culture, and the Umayyad leaders saw an intense threat in that culture. They therefore adopted an anti-Iranian Arabization policy in an attempt to suppress the nobility, language, and religion. Even common people started to be banned from engaging in traditional cultural behaviors. Such actions led to widespread dissent and discontent.[51]

The Umayyads only worsened the situation by appointing controversial Arab governors who applied their own restrictions to their populations. Governor Al-Haijaj ibn Yusuf, in particular, used force to ban written and spoken Persian not only is his court, but also for the general


[49] Hawting, *The First Dynasty of Islam.*
[50] Halm Heinz, *Shi'ism*, (Edinburgh: Edinburgh University Press, 2004).
[51] Susanne Enderwitz, "Shu'ubiya" in *The Encyclopaedia of Islam*, vol. 9, pp. 513–514 (Leiden: Brill Publishers, 1997).

population. Historians even note that the actions of al-Haijaj caused the death of the unique Khwarezmian language, a dialect related to Persian. What did the governor do? When the Umayyad Empire expanded into the east Iranian Khwarezm, he ordered the execution of any person literate in the language, leaving behind only the illiterate.

Such actions made the Umayyad Caliphate supremely unpopular, particularly among other non-Muslims who experienced similar treatment. Support for the Abbasid Revolution became widespread throughout the early 8th century , and only worsened after 741. That year, the Umayyads decreed non-Muslims could not serve in any government posts, particularly ones that would have placed them in a position of power over Arab Muslims. To avoid making the same mistakes, the Abbasids tempered their policies so they possessed a Muslim character while still appealing to the non-Muslim majority.[52]

In order to gain popular support, the Abbasids needed to diversify their tactics and operate behind the scenes until they were able to drum up the manpower and resources required to take on an empire as large as the Umayyad Caliphate. When it came to the military, the Abbasids strove to create ethnic and racial equality by mixing individuals of different backgrounds in the same regiments. These orders were passed among the influential commanders. Historians have evidence that generals like Abu Muslim recruited officers of diverse backgrounds along the silk road and registered them based on location instead of ethno-national affiliations. Doing so diminished tribal and ethnic solidarity, and created a sense of communality among the Abbasid soldiers.

This commonality would be one of the Abbasids' greatest assets as it allowed them to appeal to a broad range of individuals throughout the Umayyad Caliphate. Every group that had complaints about the Umayyads found themselves supporting the Abbasids because they seemed to target some of the problems inherent in Umayyad society. In particular, the Abbasids painted themselves as champions of ethnic equality who would overturn the imbalanced society of the Umayyads.

Of course, the Abbasids would not have been able to sway so many ethnic groups without using one of the most powerful tools in all of history – propaganda. Historians believe the Abbasid Revolution is one of the most significant examples of early medieval propaganda and its effectiveness in toppling empires. The Abbasids were familiar with the powers of subliminal and liminal persuasion and were particularly effective at utilizing symbols. For example, the Black Standard, a traditional flag believed to have been flown by the prophet Muhammad, was unfurled openly at the start of the revolution. This carried with it heavy messianic overtones since Muhammad's family had started numerous failed rebellions.

---

[52] Aptin Khanbaghi, "The Fire, the Star and the Cross: Minority Religions in Medieval and Early Modern Iran," *International Library of Iranian Studies*, (London: I.B. Tauris, 2006), p. 19.

Tugging at religious heartstrings did not end there. The Abbasids were descendants of Muhammad's uncle Al-'Abbas ibn 'Abd al-Muttalib, and they held violent historical reenactments of the murder of Muhammad's grandson by the Umayyad ruler, Yazid I. After the displays, they promised retribution. It should be noted these techniques did not focus on just what the Abbasids intended to do once in power, but instead focused on the legacy of Muhammad's family. They played intensely on concepts of messianism and religious persecution, and even revised preexisting Muslim chronicles so there was more emphasis on the relationship between Muhammad and his uncle. They wanted power, and the Abbasids were willing to fight outside of the battlefield to get what they wanted. All told, historians estimate there were over seventy professional Abbasid propagandists spread throughout Khorasan alone. These seventy worked under twelve central leaders who reported directly to the Abbasids.[53]

Further, the Abbasid Revolution relied heavily on secrecy, a tactic that was absent in other unsuccessful rebellions against the Umayyad Caliphate. For example, while the Shi'ites and other rebellions used publicly known leaders and made clear demands, the Abbasids hid everything. Few people knew their plans, identities, or even existence. Even the man who would be the first Abbasid caliph, As-Saffah, refused to become public and receive his pledge of allegiance from the people until the Umayyad nobility were executed. The Abbasids took no chances.

The military leaders followed the same policy of secrecy. The most famous commander, Abu Muslim – full name Abu Muslim al-Khorasani – used a mysterious title that gave no meaningful information. When translated, the name literally meant "father of a Muslim from the large, flat area of the eastern Muslim empire."[54] Modern historians still have no clue about his actual identity, even if they all agree Abu Muslim was a single individual and not a series of generals operating under the same name.

Finally, the Abbasids relied upon ruthlessness and deception to eliminate the last of the Umayyads and claim total control over Khorasan and the rest of the former caliphate. They tracked down any remaining members of the Umayyad family and offered them pardons if they pledged loyalty to the Abbasids. Eighty Umayyads went to Jaffa expecting to be given amnesty and were instead massacred in a brutal public ceremony. The victors would go on to desecrate the tombs of the Umayyads in Syria to further undermine the former royal family.

Once the Umayyads were out of the way, the Abbasids turned on their former allies. Abu Muslim, the infamous general, was accused of treason and heresy by the second Abbasid caliph less than five years after the end of the revolution. The caliph, Al-Mansur, had Abu Muslim publicly executed at the palace in 755. This was a poor move, as Abu Muslim was admired and loved by many of the former rebels and the general public. Numerous rebellions broke out

---

[53] Bertold Spuler, *The Muslim World a Historical Survey*, p. 48.
[54] Ibid.

throughout Khorasan and Kurdistan, and Caliph al-Mansur became known for his coldness and brutality.

The Shi'ites were next. Although they had been crucial to the success of the revolution, the Abbasids commenced persecutions in earnest. This not only was done to eliminate a perceived rival, but also because the Abbasids attempted to portray themselves as being orthodox and just rulers in comparison to Umayyad excess. Religious minorities were thus deemed heretics and needed to be eliminated. Surprisingly, though non-Muslims were treated with more benevolence and were able to hold government positions, they could not live in the same neighborhoods as Muslims, leading to the diversity of Baghdad under the Abbasids. By 755, the Abbasids were thoroughly in control and there were no traces left of the Umayyads save for some family members who went into hiding.

**The Umayyad Caliphate's Legacy**

Ultimately, as the history details, the significance and legacy of the Umayyad Caliphate is up for interpretation by many historians of the Islamic caliphates and their expansion. The Umayyad Caliphate itself was characterized by incredible territorial expansion across multiple continents but was plagued by the administrative and cultural issues one can expect from trying to incorporate a diverse array of peoples and religions into a single empire. Although diverse, the Umayyad Caliphate favored Arab Muslims over all others and became known for material excess, lavish palaces, and strict societal norms.

Such an organization, however, was instrumental in the development of the first great Islamic empire. Arabic became the administrative language as well as the lingua franca across the entire region. State documents and currency lent Arabic more legitimacy and forced individuals who wanted to rise to learn Arabic if they wanted to gain any power in the region. Mass conversions further made Islam one of the most common religions in the region, which was quite a feat considering Muslims only formed less than 10% of the entire population.

To many, the Umayyad Caliphate has become synonymous with the start of the Arab Golden Age – a period of great cultural development. However, such an interpretation is decidedly modern. Shortly after the Umayyads were out of power, historians and archivists wrote great treatises on the corruption of the dynasty. While the Umayyads were seen as managing to turn a small religious institution into a dynastic empire, such a transition was seen as turning away from the rule of Muhammad. In particular, early Islamic historians believed the Umayyads had facilitated the worship of a king over the true deity, and had given in to indulgence and excess. Such beliefs were heavily influenced by the Abbasids who strove to eliminate any positives about their predecessors.

Still, there is much to learn from the Umayyad Caliphate. It was the first successful Islamic empire, and it paved the way for many more. It managed to unite territory across three expansive continents, and place Muslims at the forefront of technological and cultural development. Perhaps just as important, the Umayyads faced the kind of serious issues that arise when trying to develop a political regime out of a religious institution. The kings viewed themselves as given the divine right to rule through virtue of their blood and struggled to maintain austerity when given control over so many resources. This caliphate would obviously not be the last to do so, but it was definitely one of the first.

**Online Resources**

Other books about Middle East history by Charles River Editors

Other books about the caliphates on Amazon

**Bibliography**

Bosworth, C.E. (1993). "Muʿāwiya II". In Bosworth, C. E.; van Donzel, E.; Heinrichs, W. P. & Pellat, Ch. (eds.). The Encyclopaedia of Islam, New Edition, Volume VII: Mif–Naz. Leiden: E. J. Brill. pp. 268–269. ISBN 90-04-09419-9.

Christides, Vassilios (2000). "ʿUkba b. Nāfiʿ". In Bearman, P. J.; Bianquis, Th.; Bosworth, C. E.; van Donzel, E. & Heinrichs, W. P. (eds.). The Encyclopaedia of Islam, New Edition, Volume X: T–U. Leiden: E. J. Brill. pp. 789–790. ISBN 90-04-11211-1.

Crone, Patricia (1994). "Were the Qays and Yemen of the Umayyad Period Political Parties?". Der Islam. Walter de Gruyter and Co. 71 (1): 1–57. doi:10.1515/islm.1994.71.1.1. ISSN 0021-1818.

Donner, Fred M. (1981). The Early Islamic Conquests. Princeton: Princeton University Press. ISBN 9781400847877.

Duri, Abd al-Aziz (2011). Early Islamic Institutions: Administration and Taxation from the Caliphate to the Umayyads and ʿAbbāsids. Translated by Razia Ali. London and Beirut: I. B. Tauris and Centre for Arab Unity Studies. ISBN 978-1-84885-060-6.

Dixon, 'Abd al-Ameer (August 1969). The Umayyad Caliphate, 65–86/684–705: (A Political Study) (Thesis). London: University of London, SOAS.

Gibb, H. A. R. (1960). "ʿAbd Allāh ibn al-Zubayr". In Gibb, H. A. R.; Kramers, J. H.; Lévi-Provençal, E.; Schacht, J.; Lewis, B. & Pellat, Ch. (eds.). The Encyclopaedia of Islam, New Edition, Volume I: A–B. Leiden: E. J. Brill. pp. 54–55. OCLC 495469456.

Hinds, M. (1993). "Muʿāwiya I b. Abī Sufyān". In Bosworth, C. E.; van Donzel, E.; Heinrichs, W. P. & Pellat, Ch. (eds.). The Encyclopaedia of Islam, New Edition, Volume VII: Mif–Naz. Leiden: E. J. Brill. pp. 263–268. ISBN 90-04-09419-9.

Hawting, Gerald R. (2000). The First Dynasty of Islam: The Umayyad Caliphate AD 661–750 (Second ed.). London and New York: Routledge. ISBN 0-415-24072-7.

Hawting, G. R. (2000). "Umayyads". In Bearman, P. J.; Bianquis, Th.; Bosworth, C. E.; van Donzel, E. & Heinrichs, W. P. (eds.). The Encyclopaedia of Islam, New Edition, Volume X: T–U. Leiden: E. J. Brill. pp. 840–847. ISBN 90-04-11211-1.

Kaegi, Walter E. (1992). Byzantium and the Early Islamic Conquests. Cambridge: Cambridge University Press. ISBN 0-521-41172-6.

Kennedy, Hugh (2001). The Armies of the Caliphs: Military and Society in the Early Islamic State. London and New York: Routledge. ISBN 0-415-25093-5.

Kennedy, Hugh (2004). The Prophet and the Age of the Caliphates: The Islamic Near East from the 6th to the 11th Century (Second ed.). Harlow: Longman. ISBN 978-0-582-40525-7.

Kennedy, Hugh (2007). The Great Arab Conquests: How the Spread of Islam Changed the World We Live In. Philadelphia: Da Capo Press. ISBN 978-0-306-81585-0.

Della Vida, Giorgio Levi & Bosworth, Bosworth (2000). "Umayya b. Abd Shams". In Bearman, P. J.; Bianquis, Th.; Bosworth, C. E.; van Donzel, E. & Heinrichs, W. P. (eds.). The Encyclopaedia of Islam, New Edition, Volume X: T–U. Leiden: E. J. Brill. pp. 837–839. ISBN 90-04-11211-1.

Lilie, Ralph-Johannes (1976). Die byzantinische Reaktion auf die Ausbreitung der Araber. Studien zur Strukturwandlung des byzantinischen Staates im 7. und 8. Jhd (in German). Munich: Institut für Byzantinistik und Neugriechische Philologie der Universität München. OCLC 797598069.

Madelung, Wilferd (1997). The Succession to Muhammad: A Study of the Early Caliphate. Cambridge: Cambridge University Press. ISBN 0-521-56181-7.

Wellhausen, J. (1927). Weir, Margaret Graham (ed.). The Arab Kingdom and its Fall. Calcutta: University of Calcutta. ISBN 9780415209045

# Free Books by Charles River Editors

We have brand new titles available for free most days of the week. To see which of our titles are currently free, click on this link.

## Discounted Books by Charles River Editors

We have titles at a discount price of just 99 cents everyday. To see which of our titles are currently 99 cents, click on this link.